COMMUNAL SOCIETIES IN AMERICA
AN AMS REPRINT SERIES

CALIFORNIA CULT

AMS PRESS

NEW YORK

CALIFORNIA CULT

The Story of "Mankind United"

H. T. Dohrman

BEACON PRESS BEACON HILL BOSTON

Library of Congress Cataloging in Publication Data

Dohrman, H. T.
  California cult.

  Communal Societies in America.
  Reprint of the ed. published by Beacon Press,
Boston, which was issued as v. 2 of Beacon series in
the sociology of religion.
  Includes index.
  1. Mankind United. 2. Bell, Arthur L.
3. Christ's Church of the Golden Rule. I. Title.
[BP605.M34D63 1979]   289.9   76-42724
ISBN 0-404-60059-X

Copyright © 1958 by H. T. Dohrman.

Reprinted by arrangement with the author.

First AMS edition published in 1979.

Reprinted from the edition of 1958, Boston. [Trim size and
text area of the original have been maintained.]

MANUFACTURED
IN THE UNITED STATES OF AMERICA

Acknowledgments

To those whose suggestions and help contributed much, both tangible and intangible, to this study of a cult—to Dean Willard L. Sperry, Professor Talcott Parsons, Professor Arthur D. Nock, Professor W. L. J. Dee, Professor William C. Lang, Dr. Tom A. Lamke, Mr. Carey McWilliams, Mr. Charles H. Manaugh, and Mrs. Virginia Crawford—the author is most grateful. He is also indebted to Harvard University, whose grant made possible the necessary field research, and to Iowa State Teachers College, for typing aid. And finally he wishes to thank Mr. Arthur L. Bell and various cult members, both loyal and dissenting, whose names shall remain anonymous, for aid in obtaining intimate glimpses into the way of utopia from those who ventured along its tribulous path.

Contents

Introduction

The story of Mankind United is the story of the world of extremist American cults. It is a world populated by an estimated 5,000,000 ardent Americans, a world with boundaries extending from Maine to California, where seemingly the westward flow of America has deposited a disproportionate number of potential cult joiners. A cult of the Mankind United variety is not, as we shall see, necessarily unique to the California scene, yet something in its balmy Western clime seems to encourage this deviant species of religious expression to sprout forth. Out of this lush California foliage the author picked Mankind United as being representative of extremist cults in general. It is, he feels, an ideal example of the modern cult.

It is easy, pitifully easy, to laugh at the followers of Mankind United and call them "crackpots." Yet, in most cases they are not very different from you and me. "A fanatic," it has been said, "is merely a person who seriously practices what we only preach." He feels that there must be a better world possible than ours, and he wants to set up the machinery by which to bring about this world. He wants to bring order out of chaos, and he discovers answers in many directions. We "reasonable" people feel the same needs and hopes, but we fail to act with the zeal of the cultist. He finds the traditional solutions to the world's ills insufficient, and he proposes new patterns for the career of man on this earth.

He may think that the answer is to be found in the dimensions of the Great Pyramid; he may recommend certain dietary habits; he may support a "scientific, technocratic reorganization of society"; or he may look forward to the advent of the Universal Service Corporation of Mankind United. Although different cults vary enormously in what they require of their followers, there are many common elements to be found among cults in general, including a personality type that often finds them attractive. Many people assume that fraud, fakery, faddism, or worse are involved; they criticize the naïveté of the "dupes who fall for that sort of thing." They look down, rather smugly, on the numerous cult programs, evincing an interest in the bizarre features, yet finding the phenomena hard to understand. They ask such questions as "What makes people join 'those things'?" "What do they offer that attracts a modern, civilized person?" "What do these cultists need that our society does not provide?" and "How do these groups operate as successfully as they do?"

It is the view of the author that the answers to these questions and many others concerning the cult world lie at the level of the concrete case, and it is with this in mind that he tells the story of Mankind United.* It was, in fact, the very extremist nature of this group that made it attractive as an object of study. As one California cult that burst forth, flourished, and then gradually withered, having a life cycle of about twenty years, Mankind United had little permanent impact on American society, but as a model of an economic-religious-utopian cult, it affords us an excellent intimate case study. Its history; its structure; its operations; and most important of all, its followers, in terms of their personalities, their lives, and their motivations—these are the ingredients for an ideal type of extremist cult that is useful as a standard for comparison or contrast.

The term "cult" is difficult to define. Certainly it is not the

* See Appendix A for Notes on Theory.

intention of the author to imply anything derogatory by the use of the word. *Here the concept "cult" will refer to that group, secular, religious, or both, that has deviated from what our American society considers normative forms of religion, economics, or politics and has substituted a new and often unique view of the individual, his world, and how this world may be attained.* It is usually utopian, having its vision of an ideal society; it is usually perfectionistic, stressing an inner rebirth in its members; it is usually anti-institutional, holding that a new pattern of society is needed; and it proclaims its rationality, decrying the blindness of surrounding society.

To evaluate the truthfulness or fraudulency of Mankind United, its leader, and its members is not within the compass of this book. Nevertheless, even before the final chapters most readers will probably formulate a judgment, pro or con. The author has striven for complete neutrality. Accordingly, along with the prophet of Mankind United, "The Voice of the Right Idea," Arthur L. Bell, the author hopes that the reader will not look unkindly upon those who "selflessly dedicated their lives to promulgating their vision of Mankind United."

Chapter I: *Of Myth, Miracles, and Utopia*

"MANKIND UNITED" ONE SINGLE BROTHERHOOD OF MAN—
"ONE FOR ALL AND ALL FOR ONE" WITH "ACTIONS" AS
WELL AS "WORDS," AND THE WORLD NO LONGER A HOUSE
DIVIDED AGAINST ITSELF,—BUT FINALLY ERECTED UPON A
SYSTEM OF "EQUALITY" AND "GUARANTEED SAFEGUARDS"
AGAINST THE FRAILTIES OF FALLIBLE HUMAN BEINGS,
COMPRISES THE ONLY PLAN WHICH WILL EVER END EITHER
WARS OR POVERTY. "SUCH IS THE PROGRAM OF THE INTER-
NATIONAL INSTITUTE OF UNIVERSAL RESEARCH AND AD-
MINISTRATION." *

"In the beginning, the Sponsors. . . ."

Upon reading the church pages of the Saturday papers, the
newcomer to the Southern California scene cannot help being
impressed or depressed by the variegated menu of religious dishes
offered by the cults and churches in the area. He realizes how
diverse are the religious needs of man. At one pole are the
modest notices of the Episcopal and Roman Catholic churches.

* *Mankind United, A Challenge to "Mad Ambition" and "The Money
Changers" Accompanied by an Invitation to the World's "Sane" Men
and Women* (Published by the International Registration Bureau,
Pacific Coast Division of North America, 1934), pp. 138-139.

1

At the other pole are the flashy advertising spreads, such as that informing us that a "Masked, Mysterious Dr. X" will give us access to the "Sacred Wisdom of the Ages," direct from the few remote survivors of the sunken continent of Atlantis, at seven o'clock on Sunday night at the Embassy Auditorium on South Grand Avenue. Not too far from the latter extreme lay the cult Mankind United.

The story of Mankind United begins in 1934. In that year there appeared in the San Francisco Bay area a book called *Mankind United* that described an international plot by "Hidden Rulers" to enslave mankind and at the same time sketched the counterplan of the "Sponsors" to foil this plot. This "textbook" pictured an existent world-wide organization called "Mankind United," consisting of many different "bureaus," "institutes," "departments," and "divisions." The principal research department was called "The International Institute of Universal Research and Administration." Subsidiary to it was an organization called "The International Registration Bureau." Narrowing our view to North America, and then to the West Coast of the United States, we see the "Pacific Coast Division" of this Bureau.

But the movement was not pictured as being new. Chapter I of *Mankind United* began by recounting:

> On December 25th, in the year 1875, a small group of generous and deeply sincere men and women met for the purpose of dedicating their lives and their fortunes to the establishment of a world-wide commercial organization which would,—by its "works" as well as its "words,"—fittingly commemorate the birth of mankind's greatly beloved exemplar and way-shower—*Christ Jesus*.

These were the "Sponsors." Originally, said the textbook, there were only sixty; gradually, as the underground movement spread, their number increased to 200, comprising an "Executive Board" of "practical, successful, and widely experienced experts and authorities, selected from the agricultural, mining, manufacturing, merchandising, banking, transportation, educational and religious groups of leaders, of the world's most advanced civilized nations." [1]

The original sixty Sponsors pledged their combined fortunes of over $60,000,000, without any hope of personal profit or recognition, to their world-saving mission. They began by creating "The International Institute of Universal Research and Administration," which had as its major purpose "the discovery and application of ways and means by which the 'Golden Rule' might be 'practically' applied in all human relationships, in order that poverty and wars would no longer occur, and men might learn to live in peace and happiness, in this gloriously beautiful world home of ours." [2] The Institute declared further that "We are prepared to prove that poverty is perpetuated and wars fought 'solely' for the profit of those who control the world's financial structure." [3]

The protagonists of evil were referred to as "Hidden Rulers." Powerfully organized, they exterminated all who stood in their path to power. Hence, said the textbook, to avoid being "eliminated," the Sponsors had carried on their struggle with the Forces of Evil in secrecy. Each of those who gathered on that Christmas Day of 1875 agreed that he would never divulge the name or identity of any other Sponsor nor admit his connection with the Institute to any outsider, not to members of his own family nor to intimate friends, nor even to the courts. The success of the venture into utopia required that the Sponsors remain forever anonymous. The textbook related, "The proof that they have been fully successful in guarding and protecting their activities, is the fact that the headquarters and the identities of the Institute's founders and research experts are—'Sixty years Later'—still unknown." [4]

Between 1875 and 1934, continued the chronicle, the International Institute of Universal Research and Administration, keeping its name and operations secret, had organized secret research laboratories that had produced numerous amazing inventions and secret devices. Moreover, the Institute had organized staffs of experts in the field of human relations who had devised the plan outlined to the world for the first time with the release of the textbook *Mankind United* in 1934. Although the Research Department of the International Institute had been ready to release its program as early as 1919, members were told, the people of the world were not yet intellectually prepared to discern the truths propounded by the Institute. "Mankind's quality of thought" had not progressed sufficiently. Consequently, in the interim the Research Department "carefully checked, tested and proved the value of each of its discoveries, revolutionary mechanical inventions, policies and contemplated plans of procedure developed during their many years of preparation," [5] and to aid in consummating its program for the world, chose hundreds of young men and women from many different nations "to undergo a fifteen year part-time course of instruction under the supervision of the various members of The Institute's Research Department"—calling this group "The International Legion of Vigilantes." [6]

Truly it would not be far amiss to call the Sponsors the "Patriarchs" of Mankind United, aided in their crusade by their trusted disciples, the "Vigilantes." Their existence extended far back into the misty and mythical origins of the movement. Yet to the followers of the cult the Sponsors and the International Institute were very real. However lacking in confirmable facts this account of the functioning of a vast Mankind United organization throughout the world might have been, it helped to form grandiose visions of earth-shaking import in the minds of the cultists, who pictured themselves simply at a lower level of this powerful, world-wide hierarchy. Few of the tens of thousands of Californians who attended Mankind United meetings in the late 1930's would have been interested in the activities of the cult had they not been convinced that Mankind United was world-wide in scope, organized by the almost legendary Sponsors.

It was in 1934, related the textbook, that the Sponsors decided to emerge into public view for the first time. "All is now in readiness for a world-wide 'free' 30-day Program, during which time the Institute's well-guarded sixty-years of discoveries and carefully prepared recommendations will be freely offered to the human race." [7] At the conclusion of this "30-day Program," a democratic, international election was to be staged; if 200,000,000 people approved of the Mankind United plan, the utopian "Universal Service Corporation" was immediately to be inaugurated. But until Mankind United, "guided by scientific information," knew that "the public's cooperation is sufficient to guarantee success," it would never give the signal for the inauguration of the 30-day Program. Warned the cult literature, "If we started and failed, and our power fell into the wrong hands, it is estimated that it would require thousands of years before civilization could again be restored to law and order. . . . We must proceed with caution. . . . If even one piece of our equipment fell into the hands of present World Rulers, civilization would certainly be lost." [8]

Like other twentieth-century cults, Mankind United had a prophet who kindled the cultic "ideals and principles" and impelled and directed the cult on its meteoric career. But unlike other idealistic but perfectly practical plans for the alleviation of human suffering that had failed because they were built around "Human Personality," the only leaders the world could ever be allowed to know were the "ideas and ideals" of the International Institute. The Hidden Rulers could cut down persons but never these eternal verities. Therefore the Sponsors were unknown; the Vigilantes were unknown; the Research Staff of the International Institute was unknown. All had voluntarily acquiesced before the "constructive ideas based on the Golden Rule" to avoid the dangers of personality leadership. In early Mankind United a man of mystery, known only as the "Division Superintendent," "The Speaker," "The Voice of the Right Idea," and other names, flitted about the extensive cult labyrinth. He revealed that he used over 200 aliases, seven "doubles," and powers of translevitation in his capacity as Division Superintendent—not to deceive but to protect himself and his fellow-workers from persecution by "the war-crazed maniacs and power-mad morons who control the political and financial affairs of this planet." Adhering to the doctrine of impersonalism, he strived mightily to remain anonymous, and by and large succeeded, for until his arrest on charges of sedition in late 1942, even his right-hand associates failed to know his real name—Arthur L. Bell.

From 1919 to 1934, Mr. Bell disclosed, he was one of the hundreds of Vigilantes who had been sought out and selected by the Sponsors for their special fifteen-year course of instruction in the International Institute of Universal Research and Administration. Testifying before a fact-finding committee of the California Legislature, he said that the Vigilantes in the various Divisions throughout the world were not permitted to know the location of the conferences which they were obliged to attend or to know

the means by which they reached the places where the conferences were held. "I was sought out by unknown persons," he
stated. "I met them frequently, but I never knew their names
. . . they disguised their identity by altering their faces." [9]

As a place for Mankind United to emerge, the Sponsors chose
the Pacific Coast Division of the International Registration Bureau of Mankind United. In 1934, according to Mr. Bell, the
Sponsors verbally appointed him the Division Superintendent of
this Pacific Coast Division and asked him to choose subordinate
officials, called "Bureau Managers," and to present the cult program to the public for the first time. "I dropped all of my other
activities as of that moment and have devoted every minute of
my time since to the carrying on of this work, the Mankind United
work," [10] he announced, and a cult bulletin added, "The Division
Superintendent has 'donated' an average of eighteen to twenty-
two hours per day of his time—seven days per week—toward the
promulgation of its [*i.e.*, the Mankind United] idealism." [11]

Operating above him, said Division Superintendent Bell, was
an intricate and secret relaying system by which orders and information were transmitted from him, as top official in the Pacific
Coast Division, to his superiors in the Mankind United hierarchy,
even to the Sponsors. He testified further, "I constantly relayed
information. . . . It was picked up at our offices. . . . I received
instructions, sent through reports constantly. I merely prepared
them. . . . I don't know where they were sent. . . . they were
picked up. I was never permitted to be present when the
messages were picked up. . . . I have been permitted no personal
contacts. . . . I carried on correspondence with many different
countries, branches in England. . . . 16 or 17 different countries. . . ." [12]

"Our miraculous inventions and 'devices'"

Our Research Department and its staff of International research experts, through their perfected inventions and discoveries, are ready to prove to the most skeptical that this world plot actually exists and every effort possible has been made to carry out the pledge of these Hidden Rulers to exterminate and destroy over 600 million of the educated and religious people of the planet. Had not this movement the power it claims, their plan would have been successful, and during the 30 days which followed March 28th, 1939, millions of the world's intelligent people would have been destroyed, bombed, gassed, or poisoned, and those who escaped would have vibrating devices turned upon them that would vibrate the eyeballs out of their sockets.*

Increasingly, twentieth-century man has looked for science and technology to supply him with solutions to the whole gamut of human problems. The champions of Mankind United were no exception: to their way of thinking the Hidden Rulers employed science for Evil; Mankind United employed science for Good. Virtually all men find the discoveries of science impressive, but these cultists looked to science for miracles—that took the form of technological miracles developed by the Research Staff of the International Institute of Universal Research and Administration. In fact, to the cult mind this Staff in its secret laboratories was not only abreast of the latest technological and scientific advances; it was far ahead of the "outside" technicians and scientists. Given their zeal to thwart the Hidden Rulers and set up the Universal Service Corporation, the cultists felt a strong will-to-belief in almost anything that would aid and abet them in achieving their

* *"A Sample Talk for Those Who Invite Small Groups to Meetings,* (Prepared by the "Publicity Committee" of Mankind United in 1941).

goals. These miraculous inventions and devices were one of the means, perhaps the chief means, by which the Mankind United Forces of Good would triumph.

Hence, amazing inventions existed, and since 1934 the International Institute could have released them to the public, but the people of the world were not yet mentally conditioned to accept the Mankind United program. In the meantime the Sponsors had employed delaying tactics, numerous times secretly utilizing their inventions to stave off the reign of terror plotted by the Hidden Rulers. Prior to World War II it was believed that the Sponsors, stepping in and using their secret weapons, would be able to end any war that might come. Appealing to the cultic imagination, stories about these inventions re-echoed throughout the Mankind United cosmos, adding credence and plausibility to the myth of the Sponsors. Being obscure and enigmatic, these accounts are hard to pin down.

Almost universally believed in by the cultists was a secret device to be given to all Mankind United co-workers by the International Institute during the 30-day Program, which, attached to their radios, would enable them to listen to Mankind United programs inaccessible to any outsider. Neither was it possible for the Hidden Rulers to block out this signal. Using this gadget the Sponsors would convey to their followers secret information concerning the various tasks to be performed, much of it through a secret code contained in the textbook, which code would then be revealed to them. Referring to this secret device, a former member told the Tenney Fact-Finding Committee of the California Legislature, "Everybody was very much enthused on that idea . . . in fact, as I say again, that was really a high point in inducting people into the affiliation." [13]

A key weapon in the arsenal of Mankind United was a device

by which all motors could be stopped—airplanes in mid-flight, tanks, trucks, automobiles, or other vehicles. It suspended all animation, yet it was not bulky. One of the Bureau Managers told a U.S. Military Intelligence Officer posing as a prospective convert that "the leader of his organization had a peculiar 'seeing eye" which he could strap to his arm, and when he raised his arm all animation would be suspended, no guns could be fired—therefore there could be no war. . . ." [14] Similarly, a cult pamphlet gave its word that, when the 30-day Program was ushered in,

We will at that time prove that mankind already possesses the ability and inventive genius to render "impotent" any and every weapon of war which depends upon any form of explosive for its destructive power . . . whether bullet, shell, bomb, or torpedo. . . . We will, at that time, also prove that facilities already exist for placing any number of armed men under a condition approximating that which is described as "SUSPENDED ANIMATION" . . . and for a sufficient period of time to completely disarm them . . . yet without in any way causing them physical suffering or bodily harm. Also we will then prove that inventions already exist which could cause the simultaneous disarming of mankind's armies, navies, and air forces, by demonstrating the fact that such inventions could otherwise be used for producing an INSTANTANEOUS AND SIMULTANEOUS explosion of munition dumps and other supplies of explosives throughout every nation on our planet (by the co-ordinated action of a few million trustworthy persons) before such materials could ever be used for the "BUTCHERING" of human beings. [15]

At another of his Tenney Committee appearances "The Voice of the Right Idea" allayed the usual tedium by informing the lawmakers that the Sponsors had twice sent him to China as well as to other places on the globe. What was unique was their method. "You won't believe me," he said, "but it never takes me more than three hours to get any place in the world." [16] His magic-carpet missions frequently occurred after he had taken a drink of water or after he had gone to sleep. He claimed to have known nothing further until the work he was to do was discharged.[17] Asked whether the translevitation was the result of some mystical power, Bell answered, "Certainly not. We have more advanced mechanical devices than the rest of the world." [18]

Flabbergasted by "The Voice's" casual assurance, the Chairman asked him, "Do you expect the Committee here to believe this stuff?" Mr. Bell replied to the effect that they, mere mortals, could not understand him because they had not received Mankind United training. When the legislators reacted with a polite rendition of the Bronx cheer, Bell murmured condescendingly, "Nor can the African savage believe in the radio." [19]

The Hidden Rulers had their science-wonder devices too— of course to be used only for evil. The Division Superintendent led his affiliates to believe that "said Hidden Rulers ever since the year 1937 have been secretly engaged and are now secretly engaged in manufacturing, assembling, and installing in strategic locations throughout the world radio-controlled equipment and devices which when operated will cause the eyes of millions of people to be vibrated from their sockets." [20] In the cult world this eye-socket vibrator was one of the most widely believed-in gadgets. Fortunately the International Institute came through with a counterpunch. Testified "The Voice" to the Tenney Committee, "I have received instructions that will enable our workers to destroy the eyeball vibrating machines of the Hidden Rulers." [21]

Among the technological wonders of Mankind United should be included the colossal granite monument that, promised the textbook, was to be erected "on the crest of one of the world's tallest peaks" to commemorate the pioneers who participate in the establishment of the Universal Service Corporation.[22] Not only were the 200,000,000 men and women who first united to form the Corporation to have their names deeply engraved upon tablets of stone, but the countless hundreds of millions who would subsequently be drawn into the utopian world society during this generation were to be similarly honored. Conservatively, a half billion names might have to be engraved on the monument —a tremendous engraving job alone. Another feature of the monument was to be a "huge museum furnished with proofs and evidences of 'mad ambition,' selfishness, greed, jealousy, hate, revolutions, wars, and the countless other expressions of ugliness which constitute the 'natural fruitage' of 'man's inhumanity to man'. . . ." In other words, the monument would provide an eternal contrast between the New Age of Mankind United and the "Each-wolf-for-himself-private profit system of our present generation." [23]

But this monument will never take shape, at least not during our lifetime, for in December, 1951 "The Speaker" Bell, in behalf of the International Institute of Universal Research and Administration, issued a concluding postscript on cultic research, revealing that

Facilities which once simplified and lightened the tasks of the Vigilantes and their immediate deputies (on the surface of the earth) have now had to be placed entirely beyond their reach because of recently highly destructive developments in the world-wide laboratories of our planet's war-mongers.

Always there has been danger of these unusual facilities falling into the wrong hands, but now no further risks can be taken. Only when the Vigilantes group is engaged in tasks many miles beneath the surface of the earth, and beyond detection, can facilities to lighten their burdens be made available to them by us. . . .

No member of said research staff has appeared on the surface of our world for many years in the past, and none will do so for at least one hundred years in the future.[24]

The Hidden Rulers

If you are so utterly stupid that the early planned extermination of over one-half of the world's population, by carefully arranged revolutions and wars—conceived for the primary purpose of systematically killing off the educated and religious people of the earth, as rapidly as possible—(embracing some four hundred million educated men and women, including you and your loved ones—and about six hundred million less cultured humans)—means nothing to you, then do not waste your time reading the rest of this announcement.*

One of the most awesome and bloodcurdling revelations promulgated by the intrepid author of *Mankind United* was that of the "Hidden Rulers." He convinced the cult followers that for many hundreds of years there had existed a secret world-wide organization, composed of a small group of families possessing fabulous accumulations of wealth, who, through their clandestine operations, were the real forces behind the affairs of man. Somehow or other, however, the Forces of Good got their start. The textbook explained, "Because of the disobedience some centuries ago of representatives and satellites of those who then ruled the peoples of the earth, both the influences of 'education' and the 'Christian Religion' were allowed to start leaven human thought." Despite the ceaseless attempts by the Hidden Rulers to eradicate these "right-thinking people," they had gradually gathered strength, especially in recent years through use of improved

* *You Need Us . . . We Need You NOW!!* (Mankind United pamphlet, Jan. 1940).

means of intercommunication, such as the radio. Now the day had come when, "the only method left to the world's Hidden Rulers—if they are to succeed in retaining their control over the world and its people—is to exterminate all people who are either educated or religious. . . ." [25]

It was believed that early in the history of mankind the Hidden Rulers had organized their nefarious operations under the autocratic jurisdiction of an executive board whose members dedicated their lives and talents to their Mephistophelean goals. The conspiracy was self-perpetuating, for whenever a member of this secret board died, those remaining selected his replacement. According to the California Attorney General, Division Superintendent Bell and his followers held "that the said 'Hidden Rulers' through its members, satellites and followers are in control of every political party, government, industry, and public utility in every civilized nation in the world. . . . That all revolutions, wars, and poverty have from the beginning of time been deliberately planned and caused by said Hidden Rulers in furtherance of their design to pauperize and enslave the world." [26] As living beings, past and present, these personifications of the power of Evil imparted a fearful reality to the world drama.

The Hidden Rulers had obtained monopolies over the principal resources of the earth, especially focusing their attention upon gold and silver; hence they were sometimes equated with "Money Changers." By dominating the financial structure and money exchanges of every nation, they have also been able to control the various governments. At opportune intervals, they cut off the flow of credit to farm and industry, manipulate the stock and bond exchanges, instigate crises and unemployment, and bring about conditions of dire need for 97 percent of the population—in other words, deliberately precipitate depressions.

Why? On the ensuing "bear" market they call in mortgages and loans, foreclose on property, and buy other property at a fraction of its worth, through these manipulations "stealing" the most desirable homes, businesses, farms, etc., from the mass of people in the world. "The only 'Trinity' to which they ever bow down," said the textbook, "is 'Money,' 'Power' and 'Influence.'" [27]

Early in their research the Sponsors had wondered why so many practical plans to prevent wars and poverty had failed. They soon learned that the vast wealth of the Hidden Rulers enabled them to destroy any movement likely to bring about a better world. These subversive forces resort to four methods to exterminate any and all opposition to their reign: (1) Intimidation, through the avenues of ridicule or direct threats; (2) bribery, of the originator of any new plan; (3) flattery, or "wining and dining" the leader of the opposition until he becomes engrossed in self-adulation and forgets his plan; (4) assassination, by the Hidden Rulers, of the leader of an opposing movement which has gained too much headway.

Very early, too, the Sponsors had learned that "the secret-service departments of the world's Hidden Rulers contained considerably over 10,000 highly trained and well-paid spies" whose sole job was to ferret out any opposing Forces of Good.[28] However, since the leadership of Mankind United had remained anonymous, relying on impersonal ideals and principles, the Hidden Rulers had no way to cope with it.

The Sponsors predicted two world wars: the purpose of the first war was to test the "potential slaughtering capacity of the war machinery," develop "fear and hate-generating propaganda," and pauperize mankind. Then in a second world war, the long-prophesied Armageddon, all "good" people would be liquidated.[29] Within six months after the end of World War II, the "insanely ambitious moral idiots" and "swinish Money Changers" were planning first to slaughter more than 400,000,000 people, including all persons who could read and write and all members of the middle classes, and then to enslave 1,000,000,000 of the remainder.[30]

To determine the relative commitment of a cultist to the Mankind United creed, one need only to query him on his view of chapter VI of the textbook, entitled "40,000 PRINCIPALITIES—ONE THOUSAND MILLION SLAVES." This chapter informed the reader that the International Institute of Universal Research and Administration possessed photostatic copies of plans (to be displayed during the 30-day Program) proving that the Hidden Rulers are plotting to set up a World Slave State, a caste system like that existing between the "Rajahs of India and their starved illiterate masses." There will be four levels of society: First level—the men and women drudges, illiterate, performing only the lowest menial tasks. Second level—the technicians, i.e., men and women slaves taught only to operate machines. These are literally "human automatons." Third level—80 percent will be a police force willing to use any brutality to compel obedience to the Rulers. Twenty percent will be the so-called "intelligentsia," conducting laboratories supplying luxuries and various needs to the Rulers. Among these will be students who, when desired, must act as companions to the Ruler and provide him entertainment. Fourth level—the 40,000 Hidden Rulers. Each of these, with his family, will rule over a principality.

Among the 25,000 slaves serving each Hidden Ruler no marriages will be allowed. However, after each Ruler appropriates the most attractive young girls for his own harem, his 1,000 student-companions will have second choice, drawing by lot whichever girls they may desire as their concubines. "All male children will be emasculated, with the exception of the healthiest and best specimens. These will be selected and trained to replace the educated members of the third group, as said members are retired from active service, or die." [31]

To keep his slaves under immediate observation and control, each Hidden Ruler will have a huge building constructed. Let the textbook describe it:

. . . these people will all be housed within one gigantic structure of twenty-five stories in height, and with the palace and gardens of its owner constructed on the top thereof. Directly beneath the ruler's palace, occupying the twenty-fifth (25th) down to and including the tenth (10th) story of each structure, there will be constructed the numerous laboratories, testing, experimental and research bureaus; television and radio departments; power-control rooms, and education center, as well as the amusement auditoriums for those comprising the third group. From the ninth (9th) story down to and including the first floor, will be located the machine shops and work rooms of the twenty thousand (20,000) slaves of the first two groups, who will be supervised by the five thousand (5,000) members of the third group, in preparation and production of food, clothes, machinery, amusement paraphernalia, and the general luxuries ordered by the ruler for his use and that of the various members of the third group whom he may, from time to time, favor with some expression of his appreciation for their loyalty and services.

The living quarters for the twenty thousand (20,000) slaves comprising the first two groups, will be located for a distance the equivalent of ten stories directly beneath this gigantic structure. They will be so placed, in order that the ruler might—by merely pressing a button,—release any one of a number of kinds of poisonous gases, and thereby not only succeed in quelling any general uprising, but also readily eliminate any of the group who might become particularly unruly. Such ones could be readily slaughtered by housing them in any one of a number of different sections of the subterranean area of his palace. In this section there will also be located the power plants, water reservoirs and storage rooms, hermetically sealed off from access by any other than the ruler's most trusted slaves.

The living quarters above referred to will contain only the barest requirements for sustaining human life. With the exception of the most attractive girls who may be chosen by the ruler and the one thousand educated members of the third group for their respective harems, the remainder of the men and women slaves in these first two groups will have their mentalities regularly dulled through the use of drugs and dope placed in their food and drinking water, in order that the quality of their thinking may remain on a similar level with that of the dullest and least intelligent creatures of the animal kingdom, and that they may therefore be readily satisfied with the coarsest kinds of food, —little or no amusement,—and a stall with some straw upon which to lie, as the only home they will ever know, or even have enough imagination to desire.

The twenty-five thousand (25,000) slaves and guards, belonging to each of those who will comprise the world's ruling class of forty thousand (40,000) men, will be constantly under the direct observation of their respective ruler, through the use of remotely-controlled television and radio equipment, microphones, television screens, etc., placed in every room and corner of the great structures which will constitute the palace as well as factories and slave quarters belonging to each ruler. At any time of the day or night, by either pressing a button or turning a dial, the ruler will be able to look at or listen to any one of his entire allotment of twenty-five thousand (25,000) slaves.

With the exception of his most trusted body-guards and himself, none of his slaves will be allowed to understand the use of guns or other armaments or facilities with which he will keep himself protected. In order that not even one of the forty thousand (40,000) rulers or their descendants may ever be tempted to increase the number of his slaves, or to gain control of any other principality or part of the earth or its resources, than that which has—by majority vote—been allotted to him, it has been mutually agreed-upon by those who constitute the

present "Money Changers" and "Hidden Rulers" of our day, that if any one of their number should yield to such a temptation, such a one and his entire unit of slaves will be blasted off the face of the earth by the immediate simultaneous attack of the thirty-nine thousand nine hundred and ninety nine (39,999) other rulers, with a combined armed force consisting of whatever proportion of their one hundred and sixty million (160,000,000) body-guards they may require for the accomplishment of such a result.[32]

This then was the terrifying pattern of life from which Mankind United struggled to save the world.

Notes taken at cult meetings before World War II portray the ominous frame of the cult mind. Discussion revolved around such topics as how the Hidden Rulers financed and prepared revolutions, sometimes under the guise of establishing world brotherhood (as in Communism), and how they carefully selected each dictator—Nazi, Fascist, or Communist; in fact, "They control secret societies, which form provisional governments and turn all political and social upheaval to the profit of the subversive forces. The Hidden Rulers are at the *very* root of all troubles, all perturbations, all conflicts, all revolts of the modern world. . . . They spoil, corrupt, decay, corrode, vilify, and debase everything they touch." [33]

When World War II broke out, the meetings re-echoed with opinions that it was a "phony" war, not actually between nations, but "conducted with the mutual consent of the actual rulers of every nation against the educated and religious classes." [34] Divulging the secret information supplied to him by the Sponsors, Division Superintendent Bell apprised a California legislative committee that "Hitler knows where Churchill is twenty-four hours a day. Churchill knows the same about Hitler. Would the people not destroy their leaders, if this war were not a racket?" [35]

The "useless slaughter" perpetrated by "moral idiots" loomed prominently in the cult literature, and Mankind United alone proposed to "do something about it." When the cult was assured of ample public support, the International Institute of Universal Research and Administration would bring into operation its secret inventions and confound the international war lords and their plans.

"The forces of Good and Evil have never fought as they are fighting now." [36]

"Heaven here and now—The Universal Service Corporation"

Swiftly, and without effort the two men climbed to the top of "an exceeding high mountain" and there, upon a vast plain far below them, appeared an awesome sight. Behind a great impregnable wall lay a beautiful city of gracious homes, spacious gardens, schools, churches, shops, factories, stores, everything for happy and contented living. A large luminous sign which hung above the city read, "THE CITY OF BROTHERHOOD" and "THE UNIVERSAL SERVICE CORPORATION." Before the wall was a group of Valiants making ready to open the great gate of the city to bewildered, suffering humanity.

Advancing at fearful speed upon the city appeared an awful figure, a great GREEN MONSTER with blood-drenched hands, large glittering teeth and terrible eyes, breathing death and destruction. WAR, accompanied by his followers Greed, Hate, Fear, Lust, Love of Money, Famine, and Pestilence, was driving relentlessly on to keep the people from entering the city. . . .

"Who are those people at the wall?" inquired Mr. Average Citizen. "They don't seem to be able to open the gate."

"You know them well, my friend—look at them closely," was the reply. Mr. Citizen studied the Valiants at the gate. Each wore a beautiful shining emblem as a shield upon his breast. On

a deep blue background, etched in lines of gold was a symbol of
the world, upheld by the clasped hands of Brotherhood, and
lettered in gold around the circular edge, the words "Mankind
United." *

"Join the Valiants at the gate!" "Become a 'Pioneer' in the
New Age!" "We must be so well-trained that we will be able
to step out of the profit system and do the work of the New
Order!" Repeatedly cult bulletins besought the co-workers in
Mankind United not to lose the vision of their approaching goal.
They were in the vanguard of those about to unveil the Golden
Age to a suffering humanity. Their task now was to set an ex-
ample for the rest of the world by applying thoughts of Justice,
Love, and Truth to all their activities. "We can now mentally
see the beautiful city that lies before us. . . ." they were told.
Aided by large, colored illustrations, the bulletins likened this
Heavenly City to a Shangri-La such as that described in the
above quotation.

It was all to begin with the 30-day Program of revelations
and recommendations that lay prepared and waiting for accept-
ance by the world. Early cultic thinking maintained that the
Sponsors would publicly release the Program when the Pacific
Coast Division filled its required membership and financial
quotas. Since these quotas were repeatedly short, the date for
the Program was postponed to December 25, 1951, when all the
inventions, devices, and discoveries of the International Institute
were to be offered free to the people of all nations, no matter
how backward they remained and despite their human failings.
And the release must be sudden, "within one-hour's time," so
that the Hidden Rulers would have no opportunity to put their

* *The Valiants at the Gate* (Mankind United pamphlet, March 25,
1942).

evil forces into the field to counterattack and destroy the Mankind United demonstration. In two-hour programs, repeated day and night, twelve times each twenty-four hours, five days a week, for thirty days, in all languages, these recommendations were to be broadcast. Every modern technique of presentation was to be used—motion pictures, radio, charts, statistics, pictures, classes, etc.

At that time the trained Mankind United members would assume the role for which they were preparing—that of "Instructor" and "Election Supervisor" for the International Institute of Universal Research and Administration. They would become the "Way Show-ers" to the rest of the world. "Irrefutable proof" would be given to a world-wide audience of one-and-a-half billion that the Universal Service Corporation was their lone hope of salvation. This thirty-day period of instruction would culminate in a democratic election to be conducted in all countries under the supervision of the numerous Divisions of Mankind United. The required 200,000,000 people were virtually certain to favor the Program because of its appeal to educated and religious minds, and from that time on, millions of those who still doubted, gradually seeing the light through their blindness, would flock to join the venture into utopia. By the end of ten years, according to the textbook, at least 800,000,000 workers would be in it. But right now, vigilance, effort, and money were required, they were told, "Our trained workers are outnumbered one thousand to one; therefore, we will make but ONE bid for World Peace—just one. *We dare not fail.*" [37]

The Sponsors, the Vigilantes, Division Superintendent Bell, and other leaders of Mankind United, still operating secretly behind the scenes, would lead in ushering in the New Age. The whole process would take only a few months. However, im-

mediately after the formation of the Universal Service Corporation, an Executive Board was to be elected to govern it. Naturally, nobody would know, but perhaps some of the Sponsors would be chosen to the Board. To keep out nepotism, each incumbent would remain in office only three years, after which a successor would be elected. It should be remembered that personality leadership was to be avoided, and inasmuch as the Research Staff of the Institute had worked on the Corporation setup for over sixty years, there should be no doubts concerning its smooth, automatic, completely foolproof operation. "The eternally good,—and by agreement—permanently unchangeable nature of a set of by-laws irrevocably wedded to the Golden Rule and the great universal and changeless laws of God,—to which Christ Jesus referred in His teachings which men have named 'The Sermon on the Mount,'—constitute the 'One and Only Form of Leadership' which will ever bring war and poverty to an end in the lives of men." [38] These would be the immediate benefits bestowed upon mankind:

(1) Guaranteed immediate employment: within one month after the 30-day Program, the Universal Service Corporation would be hiring the unemployed men and women of all nations, "at the rate of considerably over two million people per week." Furthermore, a system of "constant rotation in office" (one- to three-year terms for all official positions), with advancement based solely on merit, "without having to wait for some one in an advanced position either to die or voluntarily retire . . . as they now have to do under our present economic ('lack of') system," was to be the "permanent and unalterable policy of this great co-operatively owned service corporation."

(2) An international labor schedule of four hours a day, four days a week, for eight months out of each year: this was to apply to all types of labor: skilled, unskilled, office, and official. It would go into effect within a year after the 30-day Program.

(3) An assured vacation period (with pay) of three days a week and four months a year for all workers.

(4) A minimum salary of $3,000 a year* for all adults, both men and women, regardless of race, creed, color, class, profession, or vocation. Each "co-owner" of the Corporation would have to sacrifice his "precious egotistical belief in his own superiority" and the idea that he "deserved a greater share of the world's good than his fellows" and accept the "same-sized guaranteed pay-check." This is the essence of the economic application of the Golden Rule: a system of "Absolute Economic Equality."

(5) A pension of $3,000 a year for all men and women over forty years of age who had worked a total of at least 11,000 hours for the Corporation. (This was not mandatory; they could continue to work if they wished to do so.)

(6) A pension of $3,000 a year, without restrictions as to length of employment, for all incapacitated men or women and for all persons over sixty years of age.[39]

Mankind United asked its co-workers to recall that "less than one one-hundredth part of the fertile soil on our planet has ever been plowed," but in this New Age, "within less than one year, the world can set into motion the necessary machinery and busi-

---

* These amounts were figured at 1934 dollar-values.

ness facilities for producing over one hundred (100) times as much food and clothing materials each year as the entire population of our planet could even hope to use." [40] Moreover, "This quantity of mass production could continue for millions of years without ever even starting to exhaust the last of our planet's resources." [41]

To destroy forever the power of the despicable "Lords of Gold and Silver," who care little that "five hundred million other human beings will go hungry each day and that thirty million of them will starve to death during the following twelve months," a new form of Corporation currency was to be put into circulation. This was to be based on "Service" rather than "Gold or Silver"; everyone was to be paid in "limited-use money," which, when accumulated would be of no value, and would have to be spent by the person to whom it was paid. [42] And most important of all, within ten years after the formation of the Corporation, each employee, from the lowest to the highest, would be receiving not less than $30,000 per year, with a correspondingly enhanced good life.

Instead of piling up gold and silver, Mankind United would build manifold factories and produce enormously more food, clothes, and homes than we do at present. Every family in the world would possess a beautiful, air-conditioned home, valued at $25,000 (prewar price level). In it was to be every imaginable gadget and device for making living most enjoyable, including the finest radio, television, and motion picture equipment. Each family estate would have fruit trees, vegetable gardens, a hothouse, athletic courts, a swimming pool, playgrounds; in fact, whatever might be desired, all set amidst a landscape of fountains, miniature waterfalls, shrubbery, trees, and lawns. "Can you picture the endless miles of beautiful parks and tree-lined highways; the thousands of little artificial lakes and man-made streams—in otherwise arid sections; the playgrounds, athletic fields and recreation centers which would provide opportunity for the constructive and happy use of leisure hours, if all the world's 'hungry' people were employed for the purpose of achieving such results?" [43] the textbook asked. To relieve manual drudgery, the Research Department reported that it had discovered 100,000,000 gardeners in China, Japan, and certain countries of Europe who loved the soil and would consent to be distributed throughout the world to work these estates and parks.

An "International Auxiliary Language" was to be taught in addition to one's mother tongue, enabling educated people of every land to correspond and converse with one another and consequently promoting a closer feeling of universal brotherhood. Of course, education would be universal, and when the one language gained widespread use, most of the instruction would be carried on by radio and television courses that would emanate from one great central Department of Education. During the many vacation periods, all persons would be afforded with free transportation to assorted pleasure resorts all over the world, where they might enjoy themselves free of charge. Since there would be no cause for fear, envy, jealousy, and hate, which cause the greater part of man's physical ailments, practically all mental and physical diseases would become a thing of the past.

It is palpable that there would be no more wars; the Corporation would bring about a "world-wide demand that the world's armies and navies be disbanded," and all armaments would be "dynamited and blown to the bottom of the seas, where they will no longer menace our civilization." In the New Age a world-wide militia would be established, "with which to maintain law

and order, and with which to permanently prevent either revolutions or wars from ever again occurring on our earth." [44] In brief, the world would be *one*, and every natural and technical resource would be devoted to producing complete harmony and happiness for mankind.

Actually, few of the concepts concerning the Universal Service Corporation were new; practically all of them had been outlined in the two books, *Looking Backward* and *Equality*, written by Edward Bellamy almost a half-century before. But Mankind United went further and devised a concrete version of utopia, albeit very generally, using the sundry myths of the Sponsors, the International Institute, the miraculous inventions, and the Hidden Rulers to bulwark its program for the future. The ideal had been made concrete on paper; here was the only "practicable application" of the Golden Rule.

When the cultists discovered that the Kingdom of Heaven was immediately available and when they dedicated themselves to its realization, they felt they were doing something meaningful and worthwhile, often for the first time in their lives. "We do not have to wait for thousands of years for further evolution to take us into it, but 'today' mankind should realize the Heaven that is *here and at hand*." [45]

Chapter II: *The Pacific Coast Division of the International Registration Bureau of Mankind United*

The Pacific Coast Division of North America, is the only branch of The Institute's organization which is authorized to publish information of any kind whatsoever, relative to either The Institute or its Vigilantes. This branch is operated under the name of The International Registration Bureau, and any printed or written statements not emanating from such Pacific Coast Division, and duly copyrighted under the Laws of the United States of America, are wholly unauthorized and spurious.*

The Heavenly City of Mankind United began as an amorphous thing and gradually took shape, altering "at the command of the Sponsors" speaking through Division Superintendent Arthur L. Bell. Its Pacific Coast Division was always changing and always enshrouded in a miasmic cloud of secrecy. When queried concerning the world-wide parent organization, the International Registration Bureau, Prophet Bell proclaimed his oath

* *Mankind United*, pp. 57-58.

28

to secrecy and referred the questioner to the book *Mankind United*, where, he asserted, a full description was to be found. However, descending from the nebulous sphere of the textbook to something more finite, we have employed the term "Mankind United" to refer to the cult organization, composed of volunteer members, that stretched along the Pacific Coast from thriving outposts in San Diego to the twin capitals in Los Angeles and San Francisco to northern colonies in Oregon.

Mankind United first openly appeared in California in 1934 when interested prospects, mostly friends and acquaintances of Arthur L. Bell, gathered in the banquet rooms of small San Francisco hotels and other public auditoriums to hear talks by him and his early associates. At these intimate meetings the self-styled "Voice of the Right Idea" revealed that the Sponsors had called upon him to spread the gospel of Mankind United on the Pacific Coast. In line with his duties he was to put into circulation the textbook, which he offered for sale to them. Free pamphlet material was passed out. "You are part of the world's enlightened thinkers," they were told, "or you would not have been invited to this meeting."

Gradually the circle of adherents widened. Small "bureaus" were established that held weekly meetings for those who bought the book and were interested in the message it conveyed. In this early period the only requirement for membership was that one show sufficient interest in the contents of *Mankind United* to buy it. These early co-workers were urged to bring their friends, and although it took several meetings to convince some of the guests that the book was worth buying, buy it they usually did. At the outset the bureaus were simply media through which the textbook was sold. When a person purchased one, he automatically became a member. His name and address were registered with the bureau he had contacted, and concomitantly he received information pertaining to the related branch of the "International 4-4-8-3-4 Club." This name symbolized the goals and benefits toward which the cult strived: "A universal labor schedule of only four hours per day, four days a week, eight months each year, with a three day per week and four months per year vacation period."[1] The stipulated aim of the International Registration Bureau was to establish 8,000,000 of these clubs with 200,000,000 members throughout the world as "avenues of direct contact with those who read and become interested in promulgating the message Mankind United contains."[2]

Thus, Mankind United had cell-like characteristics from the beginning. Before long, however, segments split off from the cells. Out of the parent bureaus were chosen new Bureau Managers who set up their own bureaus. Initially each bureau adopted the name of its organizer or manager: e.g., in the San Francisco area there was the "George G. Ashwell" Bureau. Before long this practice was discouraged and the bureaus were given more impersonal and symbolic names, e.g., the "Beacon" Bureau, the "Ray-of-light" Bureau, the "Progressive" Bureau, and the "Faith-Grace" Bureau. To add to the impersonalism, each bureau and Bureau Manager was given a number, such as "#AA-188108" or "#22," for purposes of identification in correspondence and business within the cult.

Division Superintendent Bell hand-picked his first disciples, the Bureau Managers, from the early converts whom he considered best qualified and most likely to carry out his instructions with unquestioning loyalty. These Bureau Managers in turn appointed subordinate officials called "Captains" and "Lieutenants," who in turn organized lower-level "4-4-8-3-4 Club" meetings, usually held in the homes of their various members. It was not long before a vast network of face-to-face groups mushroomed throughout California.

As the cult spread, its bureaucracy became increasingly stable. The following hierarchy of leadership, in descending rank order of power, developed. First is given the area over which each official presided, then the principal system of titles applied to the officials during the early life of Mankind United.

AREA	PRINCIPAL SYSTEM OF TITLES
Pacific Coast Division	Division Superintendent
Bureau	Bureau Manager
District (unit)	Captain
Area (team)	Lieutenant
Section	Registrant or enrollee

In quick succession bureaus sprang up in Berkeley, Oakland, Fresno, Sacramento, Bakersfield, and other points in the Central Valley. Then the labyrinth crossed the Tehachapis into Los Angeles and environs, where ultimately it became more widespread than it was in the northern part of the Pacific Coast Division.

The first bureau in the South was the Faith-Grace Bureau, organized by Mrs. Bess Delight Comfort (a name previously given her by Father Divine at the time of her "rebirth" in his cult. She insisted on keeping it in Mankind United). Soon other bureaus branched out from hers.

During the heyday of the cult in early 1939 more than twenty-five bureaus enjoyed great success in and around Los Angeles. Typical of them was the Ruth-Ann Bureau. The Bureau Manager, who was a former chiropractor, had twenty-three Captains under him, each of whom headed a district. One of the Captains later asserted that she had commanded thirteen Lieutenants, each of whom had headed a team of at least five enrollees. In all, this Captain alone had 133 enrollees under her.[3] Even given the fact that this Captain and her teams were extraordinarily successful in their house-to-house canvassing and other recruitment, these figures indicate that membership in some Mankind United bureaus probably ran into the thousands.

Because of the ever-present secrecy it is well-nigh impossible to accumulate accurate figures on the size of Mankind United. Practically all the members believed it was a world-wide network; one testified that they had been informed at Christmas time, 1938, that their ranks numbered 176,000,000.[4] Later, at a highly publicized meeting held in the Los Angeles Shrine Auditorium on May 16, 1939, Division Superintendent Bell informed his overflow audience of 6,000 followers that "Of a total of slightly over 173,000,000 persons who were thought to have indicated a desire to become members of our audience, less than 75,000,000 have actually qualified for this privilege. Of this number only 15,000,000 are citizens of the English-speaking nations."[5] Subsequently he testified that the movement extended throughout the United States and seventeen different countries, including England, and asserted that the Pacific Coast Division "partly educated about 250,000 people."[6] The State attorneys concur that as many as 250,000 westerners at some time or another displayed an interest in the Mankind United program by attending meetings upon occasion, by reading the cult literature, or by coming into sufficiently close contact with active members to learn of the program.[7] The cult leader claimed that in 1939 approximately 27,000 out of the 250,000 were "active members,"[8] i.e., regularly attended meetings, bought books, and actively engaged in propagating the gospel of the cult. This period was the apex of cult popularity.

This growth of popularity was revealed in the mounting sale of the textbook *Mankind United.* In format a small, Fabrikoid-bound book of 313 pages, only slightly larger than the popular paperback editions of today, *Mankind United* cost approximately 29¢ to bind and sold for $2.50. A San Francisco bookbinder testified before the Tenney Legislative Committee that he had bound the following number of books during the peak years of cult activity:

YEAR	NUMBER
1936	1,200
1937	5,342
1938	41,182
1939	75,023
1940	2,000

Since other firms unknown to us very likely shared the job of bookbinding, these figures probably represent only a part of the total number published. Before the same legislative committee, Bell, estimating in round figures, testified that a total of 220,000 copies had been sold and given away. The outbreak of World War II prompted him to curtail the sale of the textbook; even so, the above figures roughly indicate the growth curve of the cult and validly reflect the era of greatest popularity—1939.

What happened at a typical district club meeting held when the Mankind United movement was traveling at top speed? By this time it had expanded its neighborhood meetings, formerly held in private residences, into store front meetings. We are fortunate to possess a minute account of one of these International 4-4-8-3-4 Club meetings, written by the Chairman, a district Captain. The meeting was held on October 7, 1939, in a small rented hall in a southern suburb of Los Angeles.

(1) The Chairman called the meeting to order, gave a word of welcome, and asked all who were not yet members of the club, but were there as guests, to raise their hands.

(2) The Captain began by reading from pages 44-45 of *Mankind United* concerning the impact that the forthcoming Universal Service Corporation would have upon the world's money system: destroying the grasp of the "world's subversive forces" forever.

(3) The Captain gave a short talk in which he recommended the reading of a book-length magazine called *The Key to the Mystery*, containing articles "all taken directly from the records, books, etc., of the subversive forces." He read a few of the titles, e.g., "Cruelty a Cult, Killing a Mania," which "tells the why and wherefor of Communism, the origin of the League of Nations and what it is for," etc. He explained that "Mankind United does not recommend this for study, but every article in this magazine will clearly show us the absolute necessity of working to get our Mankind United program put into operation." He further asserted that these articles "will make you appreciate how close these sinister forces are working . . . holding meetings regularly . . . just as intent on carrying out their plan of destruction as Mankind United is to bring our plan of perfection into manifestation."

For them to do nothing, he told his listeners, was to

play into the hands of the Hidden Rulers. He exhorted them to do their part by lending books and inviting those who read the textbook to come to these meetings. Then he asked for the names and addresses of those who might be interested in becoming active workers.

(4) A special speaker delivered a twenty-minute speech (at this particular meeting it happened to be their Bureau Manager). In it he gave the cultists the latest inside information on what was occurring within Mankind United and outside on the world scene. He had access to secret news, for he had just attended one of the central meetings at which the Division Superintendent had conveyed it to the Bureau Managers direct from higher, ultraconfidential sources. Now this news was passed along to the members.

Transcribed notes on several of these talks furnish us with a general idea of what he said. Following are several typical excerpts:

Within the next few days Mankind United will be ridiculed, condemned, belittled, by our newspapers. . . . The pioneers of any great movement for world betterment must be made of stuff which can remain firm under any strain—mental as well as physical. . . . In Europe many thousands have paid with their lives for their loyalty to this movement. . . .

In Europe our forces are at least partially successful—the war machinery is hitting on one cylinder only. . . .

If the Great Pyramid was destroyed, we wouldn't have the ancient signs to go by (to prophesy).

Our movement is world-wide. . . . Mankind United is a divine plan. . . . the only plan that is workable. All other groups hold out for spiritual help only. But we must help materially. . . . The Mankind United plan cannot be questioned.

. . . Evil and Good are almost equal now. It is for us to make Good out-balance Evil. . . . Our movement alone should be able to eliminate war—we can be successful if we get the workers.

During our 30-day Program we will prove that all armies and navies of the world are directed by one central group—the armies and navies of any one nation being mere pawns.

The Church of this day is a mockery. . . . All Christian organizations have without exception refused to help Mankind United.

(5) Next came another short talk by the Captain in which he pleaded for cooperation. In selecting those to whom they lent *Mankind United,* he told his listeners, be sure to try to choose those who will turn out to be "workers," i.e., those who would be likely to buy "centers" of twenty-five books for $62.50. "How else," he asked, "would it be possible to take care of the instruction and broadcasting program if we didn't have sufficient 'centers'?"

(6) The Captain read an excerpt from *A Proclamation for all Registrants,* commenting on the minor sacrifices of time, effort, and money made by the registrants on the Pacific Coast during the past five years and then pointing out that with but little additional effort on the part of the English-speaking people, the Universal Service Corporation might have been put into full operation in 1938.

(7) The Captain read from pages 60-61 of the textbook concerning the generous and unstinting sacrifices made by the anonymous members of the International Legion of Vigilantes in the course of their public service during the past nineteen years.

(8) Everybody present stood, read in unison from Section IV
of the *Declaration of Convictions and Intentions* to be found
on the heavy cards placed on each chair in the hall, and in
closing sang the *Battle Hymn of Mankind United*, which
follows (in part):

Onward Christian Soldiers, joined to end all War,
With the word of Jesus, taught to us of yore.
Truth, all knowing master, leads against man's woe,
Private Profit System, Christians' ancient foe.

REFRAIN—(*repeat after each verse*)
Onward Christian Soldiers, Mankind United,
Golden Rule of Jesus, leading us ahead.

Dictators must vanish, their Isms rot and wane,
De-mo-cra-cy, Christ taught, constant must remain.
This World's Hidden Rulers, Anti-Christal all,
Money crazed enslavers, Impotent must fall.

We a mighty army, armed with right ideas,
In bro-ther-hood united conquer Mankind's fears.
Love is not divided, all God's sons are we,
Out to bring destruction of World's poverty.

After finishing the official meeting, the Club relaxed into
a social hour in which, even though the deepest substratum of
rumor flowed freely, there was also much light banter and exchange of personal problems. Common people that they were,
the enrollees enjoyed this friendly fellowship when the weight
of their crusade lightened momentarily.

To envision the atmosphere of these meetings, we need only
to listen to a former Captain reminisce, "People would even walk
during gas rationing. . . . We discussed our mission to bring
about a new day all the time at these meetings. We were all

so happy! Upon leaving all would tell of the good time they had had." [9]

But this enthusiasm was not unmixed. Looking back at their earlier life in the cult, numerous ex-members complained of the picayune assignments frequently given to them. One Captain was telephoned at three o'clock in the morning and ordered to report immediately at a downtown Los Angeles bureau head-quarters, twenty-five miles away. When she arrived, she found only a routine matter to be taken care of. "You'd rush to do something, and then find it wasn't important," she related. [10] A long-successful Bureau Manager recalled,

> Bell always kept us in a state of suspense. We never knew why we did most of the things we did. If we ever questioned any of his orders, he would inform us "You don't know why this is to be done, but you will see. Trust me and the Sponsors, there is a purpose. You'll see later that this is necessary." So we did it. At the time we didn't know why. There was always the conviction that we would find out. Big things were in the making, and we were a part of them . . . and in time all would be revealed.

> Looking back now, I can see that he had superb timing. He always kept us hanging by a string, looking to the next goal that always failed by a hair's breadth from being accomplished. He always kept us occupied . . . always kept us busy, so busy that we couldn't think and place things in perspective. He always kept things coming at us: quotas, meetings, reports, funds, ba-rometers, etc. And he always informed us that it was *our* failure that held up the program. [11]

This firsthand account is corroborated by off-the-record in-structions that the Division Superintendent issued to his Bureau Managers:

> Meetings are to be arranged for two evenings a week, with enough literature assigned for reading and planned calls on other

inactives to keep them [the members] busy the other evenings of the week—(they must be kept so busy thinking about our program and working for its success that they will not have time to think of anything but this program). If any complaints ensue that they do not have the time, they might be asked if what we are requesting of them is any more difficult than the achievements of our forefathers when they carved an empire out of a wilderness. . . . We also must do our building and in the midst of a wilderness of poverty and war.[12]

This candid directive is indicative of the orders that circulated only in official circles. Undoubtedly it contains an important tenet of successful cult leadership. When Bell said, "In all your meetings with your people, never lift them up without giving them a chore, a duty to perform," he revealed one of the priestly secrets of modern cultism.

Throughout 1939 every interested follower had been urged to invite all his acquaintances to the large mass meetings held in Los Angeles and San Francisco, and the acquaintances in turn were encouraged to bring their friends. At these meetings all persons in the audience were invited to enroll. In like manner, the smaller cell-like meetings of the 4-4-8-3-4 Clubs and other section meetings welcomed all comers.

Then World War II broke out. Mankind United violently opposed it from the beginning, claiming that war was a "racket," a part of the "vicious plot" of the Hidden Rulers to enslave all mankind. Preaching this doctrine and realizing that they were treading on dangerous ground, the powers-that-be in the cult world decided that they had better screen their new converts more finely. Division Superintendent Bell suddenly sent out directives stating that the mass public gatherings would be discontinued for the duration of the war. All meetings, even those in the smallest cells, were to be much more selective. Those who failed to display a continued active interest were no longer invited. For many sessions a written invitation was required. In the latter part of 1939 orders went out that the sale and circulation of the textbook *Mankind United* was to be discontinued. Rumors explaining this action spread among the members to the effect that political attacks were being levied against the group, and consequently for the sake of self-protection the Sponsors felt it expedient to go underground for the duration of the war.

By early 1940 the cult had become a much more isolated and rabid group than previously. Money no longer came into its coffers from the lucrative profits derived from the sale of the textbook. Consequently it was necessary to develop ways and means of raising additional funds. The first of several plans notified the remaining co-workers that the International Institute of Universal Research and Administration was beginning a drive to enroll 20,000 persons in a "preliminary training program" that would enable them to be appointed "Instructors" and "Election Supervisors" during the forthcoming 30-day Program. At some time in the future, when the required number of enrollees was obtained and the Sponsors felt it expedient, the Institute would offer six special classes of instruction. To get in on the ground floor, so to speak, the followers had merely to enroll in these future classes and to make every possible effort to enroll ten other capable men or women as quickly as possible. The tuition fee was a nominal $20.00 each, payable in advance or in installments of $5.00 down and $5.00 per week. It was represented to be critically urgent that 20,000 future Election Supervisors be enrolled without delay.

As a matter of cold fact, much of the world-saving business of Mankind United was a financial struggle. Whenever the

Sponsors set a quota for the Pacific Coast Division, it usually required the filling of a pledge or completing of a "barometer" by the individual cult member. It is well-nigh impossible to delineate the cult mission apart from cult finance, so intertwined were the two. Bulletins from headquarters kept up a never-ending patter that in order to achieve *this* it was necessary to do *that:* in the same breath with sermons on idealistic principles came forth the most mundane financial exhortations.

Viewed in retrospect, the cult's financial policy displayed a basic, consistent trend. Gradually and almost imperceptibly, the Prophet placed heavier and heavier financial burdens upon his disciples. First there was only the sale of books; next came the enrollment fees; then various cult funds were set up, each of which demanded larger and larger pledges from the loyal members, until the so-called "50-50 fund" of mid-1943 required that they donate 50 percent of their gross salaries into the cult treasury. State Senator Jack B. Tenny, Chairman of the California Legislative Fact-Finding Committee, asserted that in the ten years preceding 1944 the Mankind United cult had received contributions totalling $4,000,000.[13]

What happened to the Mankind United millions? Outside of the operating expenses of the respective bureaus, which amounted to about five percent of the total donations, the money was forwarded to headquarters. There was no unified accounting system, only makeshift single-entry bookkeeping forms devised for each bureau. Division Superintendent Bell told his followers that "Mankind United is a movement so large that its great mass of statistics, daily records, and reports could not possibly be handled by one central bookkeeping department."[14] A Bureau Manager divulged to the Legislative Fact-Finding Committee that the cult collections were placed in an envelope and then "seemed to vanish." [15] The truth is that, shying away from the mails, the cult often employed a messenger system of collection. It seems that the usual procedure was for the money to be left lying on a table or desk in some prearranged place, for example, a Bureau Manager's apartment; then, when nobody was present, it "seemed to vanish," presumably being picked up by secret messengers from the International Registration Bureau of Mankind United.

It was with the rising heat of war fever in America that Mankind United began to lose ground. By 1941 the loyal core of cult followers had fallen to 11,500.[16] Members with only a dilettante interest shifted their attention to the international situation and discreetly washed their hands of their suspect diversion. The failure of the promised 30-day Program to unfold disgruntled many other followers, who thereafter concealed all evidences of their associations with the cult and supported the war effort.

Random quotations from notes of 1941 meetings disclose that those remaining inside built up an enormous psychological tension combining a dread of failure with a hope of imminent success. Even as late as December, 1941, adherents anticipated the release of the 30-day Program, by which the European war could be stopped and the United States kept out of war. The key to the whole matter lay in meeting the various deadlines, "passing this test, filling this quota." Thereupon the Sponsors, it was believed, would usher in the Program and save the world from terrible destruction. If there was a dominating sentiment that pervaded all these meetings, it was this sense of critical urgency and the millennial mission of Mankind United to save civilization.

"We're just one minute before the zero hour. . . ."

Then came the cataclysm—Pearl Harbor.

From this time onward the clandestine world of the cult became more and more secretive, and a chilling fear gripped the

Uniters of Mankind that unless they held their ranks against the evil forces of the Hidden Rulers, each of them would be destroyed. Their meetings reflected a desperation bordering on hysteria. Weakening under this pressure, the less zealous deserted the sinking cult ship until only about 3,500 remained on board in late 1942.[17]

Contributing to the ominous atmosphere was the fact that since 1939 the activities of the group had been subjected to intimate surveillance by the Federal Bureau of Investigation. Some of its agents had enrolled in the cult, others had set up dictographs at various 4-4-8-3-4 Club meetings in and around San Francisco, recording what occurred at twenty-eight meetings. Meanwhile California newspapers referred to "The Figure" behind the scenes in the upper hierarchy of Mankind United, but it was not until the sedition arrest and the ensuing trial publicity that the amazing operations of Mankind United were unveiled to the public.

On December 18, 1942 the F.B.I. swooped down on sixteen of the leading figures in the cult, including Division Superintendent Bell and various Bureau Managers, and took them into custody as violators of the Wartime Sedition Act. The defendants were accused of "wilfully and feloniously conspiring to disseminate false information and reports with intent to interfere with the war effort of the United States and undermine the morale of the armed forces." [18]

After a five-week trial during April-May, 1943, sensationally covered by the press, the Federal District Court of Los Angeles convicted twelve Mankind United leaders of the sedition charged, sentencing Division Superintendent Bell and six of his Bureau Managers to five years in Federal prison, with lesser sentences to the remaining five. The cult leaders immediately appealed their case, and after four years of legal wrangling and delays, the Ninth Circuit Court of Appeals in San Francisco reversed the 1943 conviction on the ground that an all-male Federal Grand Jury had indicted the cultists (among whom were three women), and this failure to include women had rendered the Grand Jury nonrepresentative of the community, just as it would have been had an economic or racial group been excluded.

Meanwhile, after the ordeal of the trial with its many extra financial demands, the cult sank to its nadir. Only the staunchest and most fanatical disciples of Mankind United remained loyal. Apparently robbed of its leadership, the movement might have been expected to disintegrate, and the curtain rung down on its role in the California cult theater.

But the expected failed to happen. Those who thought that the movement had been stamped out overlooked the rebounding qualities of the Prophet and his followers. Even before the verdict had been rendered in the sedition case, Mr. Bell and his subordinates had conceived a new form of organization for his group. He affirmed that he had planned to establish a church "on the side" of Mankind United for many years. "We've always been a church, although never given standing as a church," he told a newspaper reporter.[19]

During late 1943, even though the cult leaders operated in the shadow of pending prison terms, there was intense activity in the cult world while Prophet Bell laid the groundwork for the new form of his cult, the more exclusive, communal Christ's Church of the Golden Rule. Working alongside his attorneys, he busily readied the *Articles of Incorporation* and the *By-Laws* by which his movement would rekindle its activities. Taking advantage of a clause in California law that made it possible for "dummy" directors to sign the application for incorporation, one of Bell's attorneys incorporated the Church on January 20, 1944, without the California incorporating commission knowing that Mankind United leaders were involved in the transaction. Thus was accomplished the formal evolution to Christ's Church of the Golden Rule, describing itself as a nonprofit organization organized for "public, religious, and charitable purposes," and claiming all the benefits, prestige, and protection, including local, State and Federal tax exemption, which are generally granted to any organized church.

Despite the contention by "The Voice," Arthur L. Bell, that Mankind United and Christ's Church of the Golden Rule were two separate and unconnected organizations, most unbiased observers of the cult evolution saw little room for questioning the connection between the two. After evaluating the matter for many months, a Federal judge came to this decision:

Now there are so many, many references to Mankind United and the formation of the corporation in the literature which we have here in evidence that there cannot be any doubt whatsoever that the corporation (Christ's Church of the Golden Rule) is just a logical, consistent step in the development of the Mankind United program.[20]

Chapter III: *Christ's Church of the Golden Rule*

Learning to respect the power of cooperation, and PERFECT UNITY OF EFFORT, first on a small scale here in our "Mankind United" group in California, then spreading our influence by uniting our efforts with other branches of Mankind United throughout the United States, and finally throughout the entire world, we—the pioneers of the New Day—shall organize the Universal Service Corporation—and establish the brotherhood of man on earth! . . . That is our destiny! . . . AND IT CAN BE OUR JOY!!! *

Prophet Bell enshrouded his revelations concerning the establishment of the new church in an aura of mystery. Many of his surviving loyal disciples thought that the long-anticipated 30-day Program was finally to be released and the millennium ushered in. All of them felt that "something was in the wind." Just what it was few seemed to know, but the cult world buzzed with rumors, once again buoying up flagging hopes. Various officials minced no words, however, about the immediate need for money. In meetings and bulletins they pleaded, "Pledge at least one-half

* *Weekly Message* (Mankind United Publication, March 18, 1944), p. 3.

46

of your total salary or other income to increasing the productive facilities of our State group. . . . Beg, borrow, or mortgage your property. . . . No PROCRASTINATION—no resting on your oars for these next weeks." [1] The new venture of the cult to become a "Laboratory in Abundant Living" needed investment capital at once.

On June 5, 1943, a questionnaire went out to those still loyally embracing the Mankind United mission. It asked: "Could you live in close contact with a mixed group of Mankind United co-workers . . . meeting on the common ground of a mutual desire for the immediate fulfilment of the 'Mankind United' goal of world-wide economic equality? . . . Would you—(and if you are married, your husband or wife)—agree to pool your present properties and other resources for mutual strength . . . ?" [2] Also included were queries regarding present church affiliations, weekly earnings, work experience, dietary habits, and number and value of tangible possessions (car, home, business properties, etc.). During the ensuing weeks the most fervid respondents were sounded out further, and if they reiterated their dedication to the evolving venture into utopia, they were the chosen people given the "literally unheard-of opportunity" of becoming "Student Ministers" in the "training school for those who are to form the foundation personnel for our world co-operative—the Universal Service Corporation." [3]

During the winter of 1943-1944 the structure of this model utopia took shape, and by January the incorporation of Christ's Church of the Golden Rule was accomplished. In its *Articles of Incorporation* the cult defined itself as a voluntary association of citizens banded together for the following general purposes (abbreviated):

(a) To teach and promote the spiritual and religious welfare of mankind and particularly to promulgate the teachings of Christ Jesus, most particularly the economic teachings. . . . And to teach such subjects as will encourage mankind to adopt Christ Jesus' Golden Rule of absolute economic equality as the cornerstone of a world-wide and universally accepted system of all individual, industrial, business, political, national, and international relationships.

(b) To promote the spiritual, moral, and financial welfare of all mankind . . . by teaching and exemplifying worthy and righteous business methods and scientific ways of procedure based on the Golden Rule.

(c) To engage in all phases of educational activity.

(d) To engage in all types of social, economic, financial, civic, and educational endeavors.

(e) To acquire, organize, and conduct seminaries for the training of ministers and teachers.

(f) To receive donations, contributions, tuitions, and any and all forms of income.

(g) To engage in the purchasing, owning, selling, exchanging, leasing, mortgaging, and encumbering of real estate or other property.

(h) To establish branch organizations.

(i) To conduct business in any part of the United States and in any and all foreign countries.

(j) To adopt such rules or regulations as are necessary for the conduct or control of this corporation . . . subject to the approval of the Church Trustee.

Immediately after the incorporation the empire of the cult expanded rapidly. The assets of Mankind United, listed at $236,-

080.52, were transferred to the new Church. Mr. Bell, who in the meantime had metamorphosed from "Division Superintendent" to "Church Trustee," gleaned the California real estate market for bargains and purchased the sites of numerous church projects. In March, 1944, during a press interview he disclosed plans to set up a "vast all-out cooperative" that he hoped ultimately would embrace 200,000 persons along the West Coast. He also revealed that his program involved the purchase of real estate totalling more than $3,000,000.[4]

This rash of cult activity, especially the financial manipulations, again attracted the attention of the California Legislative Committee on Un-American Activities, and its chairman had the following exchange with Church Trustee Bell:

"Where do you get the money?" Senator Tenney asked.
"It comes to me," Bell replied.
"Where does it come from?"
"It comes from everywhere."[5]

As fast as new Student Ministers were signed up and money consequently poured into the cult coffers, the boundaries of the economic empire expanded. In his role of Church Trustee, Mr. Bell had ample opportunity to exploit his promotional ability and his adeptness in real estate dealings. He invested cleverly, and he enjoyed a buyers' market, for the war spiral of prices had just begun. Moreover, since he ostensibly planned to organize a system of self-sufficient cult projects, with each supplying itself and others, Bell entered a variety of enterprises, choosing his acquisitions accordingly.

Among the numerous properties stretching from the Imperial Valley to Oregon were office buildings (including the Continental Building, highest in Los Angeles), auditoriums, hotels, restaurants, dairies, numerous residences and flats, several Santa Monica beach clubs, laundries, canneries, warehouses, bakeries, garages, machine shops, iron works, farms, ranches, and a large San Francisco seminary building. A Mankind United bulletin of July 4, 1944, vaguely describing the extent of the cult kingdom, jubilantly told all cult followers:

Ask yourselves if any other church in the world has even dared to dream of achieving such a result for its members, let alone actually take the business footsteps through which to accomplish this result. . . . We believe it is the only kind of church that Christ Jesus would have considered worthy to promulgate his teachings. IN OTHER WORDS—A CHURCH OF "WORKS" AS WELL AS OF WORDS! [6]

During the next year the orbit of the cult continued to expand. By May, 1945, *Time* listed its assets at $3,400,000; estimates in local California newspapers ran as high as $5,000,000. Because of fluctuating real estate values and the lack of an integrated accounting system covering the properties of Christ's Church, it is almost impossible to estimate the wealth of the group beyond a round figure. When the Church reached the height of its success in the summer of 1945, price levels were curving upward. Conservatively, we may assume that at that time, though most of the property was heavily mortgaged, its assets exceeded $3,500,000. The following list of its real estate holdings, extracted from court records, provide a sketch of the extent and variety of the cult empire at its zenith:[7]

SOUTHERN CALIFORNIA PROPERTIES

The Continental Building (a twelve-story, steel-reinforced office building), Fourth and Spring, Los Angeles, California.
Homesteaders Office Building, Los Angeles, California.

Stratford Hotel, Los Angeles, California.

Ocean Park Bank Building, Ocean Park, California.

The West Adams Gardens (consisting of two blocks of four-unit flats), Los Angeles, California.

Santa Monica Athletic Club, Santa Monica, California.

Wavecrest Beach Club, Santa Monica, California.

Sorrento Beach Club, Santa Monica, California.

Several chiropractic offices, Los Angeles, California.

Cannery, Redlands, California.

Your Laundry, Maywood, California.

Machine Shop, Ocean Park, California.

Casa Blanca Hotel, Ontario, California.

Tip Top Hotel, Azusa, California.

Egg farm, Pomona, California.

Rabbitry, Inglewood, California.

Several trucking outfits and garages, Pomona, California.

Several dental offices, Los Angeles, California.

Several large mansions in Hollywood, California.

Numerous houses scattered throughout Los Angeles County.

Numerous lots throughout the Los Angeles area, including some valuable downtown property, one being a parking lot.

Numerous small apartment buildings, flats, and other miscellaneous buildings in the Southland.

Various fruit farms in the area.

Several mountain resort properties.

Scattered warehouses and garages.

Numerous restaurants (some connected with the above-listed hotels).

Three ranches in San Bernardino County, California.

Eight ranches in the Imperial Valley, near Brawley, California.

NORTHERN CALIFORNIA PROPERTIES

American Laundry, San Jose, California.

Creamery, Monterey, California.

Golden Rule Bakery, San Francisco, California.

Palomarin Ranch, Marin County, California.

Several sawmills in northern California.

Dairy, San Jose, California.

Laundry, Petaluma, California.

San Francisco Seminary, 801 Silver Avenue, San Francisco, California.

San Francisco Laundry, San Francisco, California.

Kean Hotel, San Francisco, California.

Hotel Cecil, San Francisco, California.

Granada Hotel, San Francisco, California.

Valuable downtown San Francisco parking lots, one on Mission Street, the other on Mason Street.

Rancho Dos Palmos, San Joaquin Valley, California.

Buri Buri Ranch, San Mateo County, California.

Numerous other ranches of varying sizes throughout the northern part of the State.

Hardware store, San Francisco, California.

Haberdashery, San Francisco, California.

Several garages and warehouses, San Francisco, California.

Iron works, San Francisco, California.

Motel, Napa, California.

A number of restaurants, some connected with the San Francisco hotels listed above.

Numerous lots scattered throughout the north.

Numerous apartment houses, houses, and miscellaneous buildings in San Francisco, San Jose, and various other northern California cities and towns.

OREGON PROPERTIES

Paradise Meadows Dairy, Eagle Point, Oregon.
Hydro-electric power plant, Eagle Point, Oregon.
Auto court, Eagle Point, Oregon.
Grants Pass Hotel, Grants Pass, Oregon.
Hillcrest Bulb Gardens, Grants Pass, Oregon.
Cheese factory, Jackson City, Oregon.
Fish Hatchery, Jackson City, Oregon.

As rapidly as Prophet Bell acquired this physical kingdom for his cult, his most trusted subordinates, operating as "Statistical Project 11-A," fell to organizing each income-producing property into a "church project" of Christ's Church of the Golden Rule. All Mankind United adherents who had responded favorably to the questionnaire of June, 1943, affirming their desire to become Student Ministers, were instructed to fill out numerous forms giving "Co-Worker Placement Data," which were intended to facilitate the assignment of cult personnel. Utilizing this data, the cult officials applied the law of supply and demand in adjusting the incoming Student Ministers to the church properties being established as church projects.

This manipulation of cult members received legal sanction from the *By-Laws* of Christ's Church of the Golden Rule, which placed absolute powers in the hands of the "Church Trustee." During the conversion period, Arthur L. Bell had received this office by prearrangement. Hence, as Church Trustee, before any application for membership went into effect, he had to stamp it with his approval; he was empowered to pass final judgment on the personnel placement of each Student Minister; and he had the power to excommunicate any of his followers from the Church. Confronted with this picture of centralized authority, a Federal judge concluded that "actually this movement was and is a one-man enterprise, completely controlled, managed, and dominated by Mr. Bell." [8]

The big push for Student Ministers to work the expanding network of projects came in early 1944. In various strategic cities on the Coast where strong Mankind United bureaus flourished, mass meetings of the good prospects were called. In Los Angeles this meeting was held at a downtown auditorium on May 16, 1944. About 500 people were present. "We were told to come there for a very, very important meeting," one who was present later said. "All the people I had ever been associated with in Mankind United were there." [9]

Versions of this May meeting vary. One ex-member who had earlier dedicated himself to the cult mission testified:

> Mr. Bell came out on the rostrum. The first words he said were "Today we are a church," and everybody clapped. Then he said—he read part of the Charter to us, and everybody laughed as he went along because it encompassed so many things. We were able, according to the Charter, to do most anything. . . . If the State of California had known that Mankind United was behind this church, they never would have granted the Charter. He said, "We really put one over on the State this time." That is exactly what he said. [10]

Others complained of high-pressure tactics:

> If we raised any questions, they told us to "read between the lines"; they said that such air-tight wording was necessary to escape the present political persecution. . . . Before we could think it over carefully, we were rushed into signing the Application for Membership. [11]

None the less, the atmosphere at the gathering was an elated one. Most saw Christ's Church of the Golden Rule as a California model of the Universal Service Corporation—a demonstration to all of mankind. "The entire world would pray for our success if it could but realize the importance of our efforts," they were told. The Prophet bluntly informed them that conditions might be primitive, but as such would be their tests: "Perhaps you will have to live in tents for awhile." And neither should they expect the Kingdom of Heaven ready for them to walk into. In retrospect, a loyal Student Minister put her feelings this way:

Well, he [i.e., Mr. Bell] read to us the Charter, and we were all very happy about it, naturally. I do remember, though, that after he had read it he said, "Now this is going to be a crusade. You are going to go through many hardships. It is a camping trip. We are testing you out to see what kind of material you are, whether you are going to be able to put the Golden Rule into application in your daily lives". . . . But I think we were all very happy and glad that we were able to start in on it.[12]

After this auspicious send-off, the new form of the cult soon built up steam and got under way. Those who had refused to sign at the May meeting were visited again and again by higher-ups who applied pressure from every angle of cultic, religious, and economic idealism. If one of the members of a family joined, he was used as the avenue through which the others were drawn in. The leaders stressed converting whole families. If either the husband or wife demurred, no means went unused to bring in the laggard.

But many who were willing to go along with Mankind United as long as they could stay in their own homes and on their jobs were unwilling to give up all their worldly possessions and subject themselves entirely to the rigorous discipline and work re-

quired of the fledgling Student Ministers. Consequently, for some
years alongside the emergent Christ's Church of the Golden Rule
a depleted network of the older Mankind United bureaus continued to operate. Although much curtailed in their activities,
these outside cultists, referred to as "The Field," secretly contributed much money to the support of the new venture before
losing faith in its mission.

Although the emergence of the Church occurred only five
years after the apex of Mankind United popularity, the ensuing
war years had screened out all but the most zealous World-
Savers. This loyal remnant, numbering approximately 850,[13]
signed the *Application for Membership,* and by this act, in the
language of the *By-Laws,* they became "Initiate Members," willing to forsake the "World" to become Student Ministers on a
Christ's Church project. In entering the Church, they agreed to
contribute all their "worldly possessions" to help acquire the
facilities for "illustrating their ministry," and thenceforth they
were considered "Children of the Church."

In the process they were completely "freed from the bondage
of ownership" of their personal property and real estate. Their
individual contributions varied enormously, ranging from $200 to
$32,000. Only a few gave less than $4,000 or more than $15,000:
the mode fell somewhere between $4,000 and $8,000.[14] Once
having signed the *Application,* they became enmeshed in the
financial tentacles of Christ's Church of the Golden Rule, and
afterwards, as those who later withdrew discovered, it was difficult to extricate themselves.

Upon dedicating themselves to the cult crusade, all Student
Ministers, regardless of rank, were required to cut off all relations
with the outside world—job, home, relatives, and friends. What
is more, Prophet Bell permitted no contacts between different

church projects and forbade fraternization among fellow members outside the particular project on which they worked. Consequently, to the newly signed initiate members the over-all configuration of Christ's Church shaped up very hazily.

Adding to the mystery of embarking into this invisible kingdom was the secrecy veiling the ultimate project destination of each new Student Minister. As soon as he had put his worldly affairs in order, cult officials operating out of Statistical Project 11-A bombarded him with a barrage of directives. Using numbers instead of names to refer to the persons and projects involved, they ordered him from place to place, lending to the proceedings an excitement and sense of adventure that contrasted with his prior life in the humdrum outer world. In the wake of these cloak-and-dagger tactics, to help him break completely with his former life, the Student Minister typically found himself placed in training far from his former haunts.

The utopian spirit of the Universal Service Corporation fired these early converts when they joined their comrades on the "Laboratories for Abundant Living." Their leader warned them that it was a "terrific test of selflessness" to give up their worldly possessions and to enter training with others who were also first encountering life in the New Age. However, they renounced the worldly life only temporarily. For the time being, as Student Ministers, they were learning to apply the Golden Rule here and now, so that ultimately the invisible network of Christ's Church of the Golden Rule might emerge and they might demonstrate to the world what practical Christianity really was. They were told:

The best way to let the world learn this dignity and joy of brotherly love and services to others, "of washing the Disciples' feet," so to speak—washing soiled linens, making beds, providing delicious food, immaculate hotel rooms,—with no thought or opportunity for personal financial gain—and doing it all with genuine KINDLINESS AND FRIENDLINESS—NOT JUST THE ARTIFICIAL SMILE THAT MUST BE PUT ON BY THE TIRED CLERK WHO WORKS ONLY FOR A PAY-CHECK AT THE END OF THE WEEK,—is to provide that LIVING EXAMPLE.[15]

Now, in their practical, everyday activities, they were being tested in the predawn darkness; soon the first rays of the millennial sun would burst forth over the horizon. Then they would emerge in their true light as "Way Show-ers" to the world.

Theirs was a communistic ideal. Underlying it was a cult metaphysics that had at its core the idea of absolute equality, "One for all and all for one." Bell once told a reporter that his concept of the Golden Rule was that "everyone should have the same size paycheck—from the President to the ditchdigger." [16] Instructions issued to initiate members stated, "And always remember, *we are all equal,* all working for the good of the whole —and the work must be harmonious if it is to be a perfect work, made perfect with the joy of working for a common ideal and objective." [17]

With these sweet phrases ringing in their ears, they expected great things when they abandoned the world, but their ensuing assignments often dampened their early fervor. They were brusquely told, "This is a crusade, not a Sunday School picnic," and as their part in this crusade, all Student Ministers were expected "to devote a minimum of twelve hours a day, six days a week, to their work on the project. . . ." [18] Included in this twelve-hour period was a maximum of only one hour for meals, but not included was the time they were expected to spend writing digests and sermons, attending special meetings, and studying official cult literature.

Ideally, according to Church Trustee Bell, all project facilities would be equal and all food, housing, necessities, even personal luxuries would be plentiful before long. Actually, the church projects varied widely. On some, life was hard; on others, comparatively easy. To keep understaffed projects operating required that the project members work up to sixteen hours a day, at times seven days a week. On other projects where there was an ample labor supply, the formula was only eight hours a day, six days a week, which, incidentally, was the lightest load permitted the trainees.

The Student Ministers received no wages nor recompense of any kind. They got their board and room, but here again there were many disparities. With food prices elevated by the war, they were expected to live on less than $40.00 a month, and on many projects the policy was to allot an average of forty cents a day for board. In addition, they received a small, so-called "gift" for incidentals, usually $5.00 a month—if their project made money. If it lost money, they were apt to receive nothing. They showed little concern for personal luxury; certainly they received little on the projects. Their clothing they had brought with them from the outer world, first giving it to the Church. Many practiced vegetarianism, but it was not required. Smoking was discouraged. Drinking was taboo.

Granted that their ascetic life was hard and frugal, yet they bolstered their morale by remembering that they had comrades-in-arms in their crusade, all working together toward perfection.

To most Student Ministers this camaraderie of the small, self-conscious community was one of the highlights of their cultic career. There was a warmth and intimacy in training together on a church project that contrasted with the cold, "dog-eat-dog" life of outside California society. Actually these "World-Savers" were

closer than many family circles. They ate together, worked together, talked metaphysics together, gossiped together, relaxed
together, and contacted no one outside of their cell of fellow
workers. In this intimate situation each Student Minister naturally took upon himself the attitudes of his associates. Stimulated
by their words and deeds, he generated an inner hypersuggesti-
bility toward the ideals and principles of the cult. He identified
his values with those of his fellows. He saw them respond as
ardently as he. He stimulated them; they stimulated him. The
product: an intensified dedication to the common, cultic mission.

It is plain that there was an enormous intellectual inbreeding
in these communities of Student Ministers. The sole contact they
had with the over-all kingdom of Christ's Church came through
the countless mimeographed pamphlets sent out from Statistical
Project 11-A. Viewed as a whole, this literature flooded their
minds with a potpourri of instructions, condemnations, congratu-
lations, reports of progress to date, promises for the future,
mythology, Christian doctrine, metaphysics, and sundry other
topics. Since the cultic answers were the true answers, there was
no need for the mutation of fresh or untried ideas. Theirs was a
closed system. They had the truth.

The Prophet and his entourage recognized the pre-eminent
function of this literature. From the top down, every official had
to possess literary talents of a sort, and since the bulk of cult
business and teachings was transacted on paper, an aptitude for
writing was an invaluable, almost a crucial, asset. Mr. Bell devoted many painstaking hours to writing his share of mimeographed tracts. They were his sermons to his flock. They were
the levers by which he controlled his movement. By chewing and
rechewing them as their daily diet of assigned lessons, his followers thoroughly digested his vocabulary, often using his very

terms and phrases. Upon one occasion he candidly informed them that any large organization travels on paper. Assuredly it was true of Christ's Church of the Golden Rule.

The *de facto* capitol of the cult empire was the San Francisco Seminary Project, located on Silver Avenue in the southern part of the Bay City. Purchased in April, 1945 for $250,000, it was a huge, flat, brick structure with over 200 rooms, including a spacious chapel, a gymnasium (converted into a weaving center with numerous looms), classrooms, lounging rooms, an infirmary, a large, central dining hall in the basement, and several dormitory wings. Ordinarily about 250 persons, Student Ministers and their families, dwelt there. Later it became the temporary living quarters for well over 300 persons. Obviously it was overcrowded.

At the apex of Christ's Church activities, there were forty-eight church projects in operation in the Bay area, eight in San Francisco proper. Many of the Student Ministers working on them lived at the Seminary, commuting to their respective training projects. Only the few who waited on the public came in contact with outsiders. As a whole, the Seminary project was an exclusive group.

The heavy curriculum at the Seminary kept everybody fully occupied. First of all, there were the Saturday night discussion meetings concerning religious topics. On Wednesday night there was a mass devotional service, at which the most advanced Student Ministers officiated, with the added attraction of a testimonial period such as that found in Christian Science. On Tuesday evening there were meetings of different cell-like committees to discuss problems and complaints. On Thursday evening there was usually an educational film or special speaker. On Friday night came the policy-making, round-table discussions at which the Student Ministers took up such project problems as details of training the children, allocation of jobs to the best qualified, and the appointment of various subcommittees. In addition to the weekly meetings, there were regular devotional services held each morning at 7:00 A.M., Sundays at 9:00 A.M. Unless circumstance demanded a special meeting of some kind, Sunday evening was devoted to entertainment or any kind of relaxation enjoyed by the Student Ministers. Some danced; others played games; others preferred to continue their discussion of the omnipresent ideals and principles.

No sluggards were allowed. All children attended a school organized on the project. Of those Student Ministers not working on outside projects, some attended to administrative detail, some taught in the school, some worked in the communal dining hall, others ran the literature and mimeographing department, others operated a candy kitchen, others worked the looms, others worked in a ceramics department, others studied typing and music, still others presided over the library, and finally, a chiropractor and his aides had charge of the project infirmary. Officials took care that everyone was kept completely preoccupied with affairs of the Church.

One of the largest projects under a single manager was the Imperial Valley project, consisting of eight different ranches near Brawley, California. Here there were thirty-six Student Ministers and a total of seventy-three men, women, and children. During the harvest seasons, if the situation demanded, the women and children aided in the field work. It is evident that the Project Manager determined the temper of the community. In this case he was a man dedicated to the all-embracing, world-saving vision of the cult, and he tried to make his project a small-scale model of his vision. He wielded his authority with prudence, countenancing no inequalities of status among his trainees. "We have

·our conferences together, we are studying our ministry together," he testified, "and that is the whole idea of this setup, to provide us with the tools that we can go out and demonstrate to the world. . . ." [19]

On the large ranches there were informal religious meetings ·after each evening meal; on the smaller, only biweekly discussions concerning problems of the project, the workers driving twice a week to several of the larger ranch houses for major meetings. Every Wednesday night the Student Ministers from the eight ranches assembled for a devotional service where, although the Project Manager was the minister-in-charge, each Student Minister in turn took the rostrum. "Each is allowed to conduct the meeting as he sees fit, according to the inspiration he gets," [20] ·asserted the Project Manager. In addition, each trainee wrote a weekly digest as assigned by the *Weekly Message* and brought it with him to the Saturday night discussion meetings, where he ·contributed his particular insight to the group thought.

Another Student Minister training project, the Tip Top Hotel, at one time might have been nominated as an ideal cult community. It was set up in Azusa, a small town near Los Angeles. The Project Manager was a kindly and easygoing man of about sixty. Probably above all else he delighted in discussing matters cult and occult. At the embarkation of Christ's Church he thought he had found the true solution to the world's ills, and it seems that he transmitted his conviction and spirit to the project atmosphere. Between twelve and fourteen Student Ministers lived and worked at this hotel project, including the Manager's wife and several daughters. There was no shortage of rooms, and since the group operated a café in connection with the hotel, the trainees fared well in matters of food.

Apparently these Student Ministers were well adjusted to

their lot at the hotel and found the intimate life quite agreeable. If one of them fell behind in his work, the others, "practicably applying Christ's Golden Rule," pitched in and helped him catch up. In short, there was a general spirit of cooperation and congeniality. One of the former members stated:

> We had a very good reputation in Azusa. We went there under somewhat of a cloud, but before we left, the people of Azusa had considerable good will toward the people of this Church. We were allowed to conduct our project in the manner in which we intended it to be operated.[21]

Others evinced a similar pride in their project accomplishments.

When they were not working at their practical tasks about the hotel, the Student Ministers devoted most of their time to studying the cult literature, which was supplied them in profusion. Intermittently they met together to discuss what they had read. Unlike some of the larger church projects, they seldom collected for hymn singing; instead they centered their attention on metaphysics and the future. Even on their jobs, their topic of conversation usually concerned some aspect of church beliefs or affairs. Little time was allotted for recreation, and outside of their own social evenings, few opportunities were available. It is evident that each project member dedicated almost his whole consciousness to things cultic.

But the mellifluous atmosphere failed to last. In mid-1944, at the height of the war, Church Trustee Bell rented several of the cult's large diesel trailer-trucks, ordinarily used to transport produce between projects, to an outside company for the purpose of hauling oil, all the while being driven by Student Ministers. Several of these drivers lived at the Tip Top Hotel project and aired the news of the renting. As a result, a rebellion seethed and finally flared up, producing one of the first schisms in cult ranks. Leading the insurrection, the usually mild-mannered Project Manager blasted Bell for playing with the God of War and prostituting the Church equipment to the "Black Captain." Several times the Personnel Manager of Statistical Project 11-A appeared at the project and pleaded with the rebels, but he failed to put down the uprising, and after a sizzling exchange of charges and countercharges, the dissenting members left the cult en masse.

Looking at the Pacific Coast Kingdom in retrospect, we see that some of the church projects were well managed; others were badly mismanaged. In some the Student Ministers were satisfied and happy; in others, dissatisfied and disgruntled. Certain projects made money; others lost money. In most cases it appears that the deciding factor was the ability and personality of the Project Manager. When rebellion broke out in the ranks, it usually erupted where projects had been mismanaged, and the local project workers felt that the proclaimed cult ideals had not been practiced. Conversely, on other projects the Student Ministers were convinced that finally they had found a worthwhile life and that they were actually living the Golden Rule here and now.

Turning now from descriptions of the "Laboratories in Abundant Living" to the matter of their relations with the outer world, we find that less than two years after establishing Christ's Church, Prophet Bell released a bombshell that set off a concatenation of events disastrous to the Mankind United mission. For some unknown reason, in July, 1945, he suddenly offered for sale nine of the largest Los Angeles church projects, valued at $1,500,000. When he failed to sell them promptly, he decided to put them up for public auction in October, 1945.

But just before the auction another factor appeared on the

scene that initiated a blow even more dangerous to his cult than the earlier sedition trial. The California Attorney General filed a complaint in State bankruptcy courts asking for the ouster of Church Trustee Bell, the termination of the activities of Christ's Church of the Golden Rule, and the appointment of a Receiver in Bankruptcy to wind up its affairs. In so doing, the State alleged that there had been irregularities in the conduct of church affairs, especially in matters financial.

Strange pleas coming from the cult world prompted the State to bring Christ's Church under scrutiny. Shortly after the church projects had begun operation, letters began to appear in the Attorney General's mail complaining of the helplessness and misfortune of the writers. Disillusioned by their experiences on the projects and describing an autocratic atmosphere of fear, bullying, and dire threats if they complained of their lot, certain Student Ministers appealed to the Attorney General for advice and aid in retrieving their donations to the cult. This group was commonly called the "dissenters." As a result of their pleas, the State assigned special investigators to their cases, and in view of the evidence collected, became increasingly interested. Finally the real estate sale prompted the State to move in and bring bankruptcy proceedings against the cult.

The State of California immediately swung into action. As soon as the Receiver in Bankruptcy had been appointed, special State agents began to take over the cult kingdom, breaking into the church projects forcibly when necessary. They met with fanatical resistance from the Student Ministers, who, mum and defiant, often barricaded themselves inside, whereupon the agents had to employ locksmiths to gain entrance.

"The Voice" was not caught napping. Within three weeks, to escape from the "malicious, anti-Christ attacks" of the State agents, Bell threw his Church into voluntary bankruptcy in the Los Angeles Federal courts, which had jurisdictional precedence over the State courts. By so doing he stopped receivership seizure of the Christ's Church properties.

From this point on, the declining career of the cult revolved around the protracted legal battle between the State and Federal governments on the one hand, and, on the other, the cult prophet, Arthur L. Bell, who liked to picture himself as "being in the front-line trenches." Inside the cult fold the schism between the dissenters and the loyal Student Ministers stirred up excesses of emotions and hatreds. Each faction sent a delegation to the court proceedings, where each huddled at its side of the courtroom, frequently glaring at the other and shunning all intercourse. All in all, this legal skirmish was waged in and out of Federal courts for more than six years—from October, 1945, to December, 1951.

Throughout this period the cult struggled along under the wraps of the court, so to speak. The Trustees in Bankruptcy assumed the financial direction of the church projects, with Christ's Church continuing to operate them and with the Student Ministers continuing to live on them. The cult leader often proclaimed and lamented that there was a deliberate plot afoot to destroy his movement through huge litigation costs, all of which ultimately had to be paid by the bankrupt estate. But more than devouring the cult assets, the protracted legal action stymied any expansion of cult activities by requiring that the Prophet direct his every effort to the defense of himself and his loyal disciples rather than to proselyting new followers.

As the proceedings dragged out, the cult gradually retreated northward and entrenched itself in the San Francisco Bay area, abandoning its southern projects under the duress of the trial.

From the first, in order to pay the skyrocketing legal costs, the Federal judge pursued the over-all policy of disposing of the projects that were running in the red financially. Consequently, there were intermittent public auctions at which these properties were sold, until finally in early 1948 the Judge ordered the liquidation of all Church properties in the Southern California area. Whenever the court held an auction and projects had to be vacated, the Prophet was confronted with the problem of what to do with the dispossessed Student Ministers, still loyal disciples, who were literally destitute and homeless. He juggled them here and there, from project to project.

As their messianic fire was slowly quenched by their legal tribulations, the cultists realized that the success of their venture required peaceful coexistence, at least for the time being, with the surrounding society. We have seen how black a picture early Mankind United had painted of the outside economic system and its sycophantic institutions, particularly the churches, that cooperated in exploiting the common people. In contrast, by 1946 the Student Ministers came to feel keenly the reactions of the outer world to their activities, and they began to strive, almost desperately, to earn the respect and approval of the community in which their project was located.

In San Jose, for example, the Student Ministers at the American Laundry project, no matter how humble their task, evinced pride in the service that they rendered to the people of the city and asserted that they had the respect of both residents and businessmen. To show their good will and also to spread their gospel among noncultic patrons, they inserted a weekly mimeographed pamphlet, *A-L the Sud's Chief, Rainbow Hues of New Age Views,* into each laundry bundle.

None the less, outside businessmen, especially those in small towns, were generally unsympathetic. In Petaluma, just above San Francisco, there was another laundry project with about thirty Student Ministers in training. When a member of the Petaluma Chamber of Commerce was asked what the general sentiment of the community was toward these cult members, he answered:

Well, I would say that the general sentiment is pretty much a sentiment of pity for them. People feel sorry for them . . . on the grounds that they work pretty hard, for which, as I understand it, they do get the religious benefits and their food and clothing. No pay, they are very poorly dressed.[22]

When asked whether there was any objection in Petaluma to the Christ's Church organization, he replied:

Well, the objection was entirely on the basis that we didn't want that type of an enterprise in our town. From a business standpoint it was not good business to have 250 or 300 people working and taking the place of our local people who were working on those projects, to come in there and work with no payroll whatsoever.[23]

Most likely this was the average civic reaction, especially of businessmen, to the church projects in their midst. In view of the predominantly secular temper of California society, it would have taken a community tantrum to bring townspeople to persecute project workers for heretical beliefs: religion is not that important to the average Californian. Local denominations simply shunned the cult. Generally speaking, the attitude of the surrounding community was that the Christ's Church people were "queer ducks," but nevertheless they had the right to think and do what they pleased.

To avoid further alienating the outer profit system and to

prevent further legal trouble, Prophet Bell once again reorganized his movement. In February, 1948, he set up a new "temporal agency" to handle the secular, business end of cult activities alongside the "Ecclesiastical Society" of Christ's Church of the Golden Rule. Aided by his staff, he drew up a stringent code of "canon laws" covering all aspects of an "apostolic mode of living" for his 700-odd remaining loyal disciples. By their unanimous vote, Mr. Bell, alias the "Division Superintendent," "The Speaker," "The Voice of the Right Idea," the "Church Trustee," was elected to the office of "Senior Elder." In putting on the frock of his new office, Senior Elder Bell possessed his greatest power ever as a cult leader.

This new monastic structure failed to revitalize the cult, however, and in the years following 1948 the cult underwent a gradual disintegration and decay. The court continued to liquidate the church projects as additional operating and bankruptcy expenses had to be met, until finally, as one former Student Minister recalled, "Everybody seemed to be fed up with it and wanted to get it over with." Finally in December, 1951, the cult officials, having paid all claims against Christ's Church, succeeded in extricating it from the bankruptcy proceedings and once again they took over complete control of the remnants of their kingdom.

A purview of this twentieth-century cult versus the outer world shows us that at first, like numerous sects in history, Mankind United attracted little attention. As it grew and prospered, however, society took notice, but knowing little about its organization and operations, continued to ignore it. Politically it was watched, perhaps apprehensively, for if it spread, it might become a voting group to be reckoned with, yet no official action was taken toward it. Then in 1939 the Federal Bureau of Investigation began to probe into its activities and shortly became more and more interested. In the mind of the Mankind Uniter this was the first overt action taken by the forces of the Hidden Rulers against the expanding Forces of Good in the world. For the ensuing twelve years the pressure from the outer world never slackened until it was evident that this movement, as a potential threat to the outside system, had gone down in defeat.

Early Mankind United, as a self-conscious crusade, brooked no accommodations to the outer world, mincing no words in denouncing the values of modern society. Society, in turn, reciprocated with a growing hostility toward this aberrant group in its midst. Utilizing the courts, it kept the cult in hot, sometimes almost boiling, water beginning with the sedition trial and leading into the lengthy State and Federal bankruptcy proceedings. Toward the end of this legal embroglio, although the outside pressure subsided, Christ's Church of the Golden Rule lost its missionary impetus and, withdrawing more and more into its private world of projects, it reconciled itself to a marriage of convenience with the outer world and adjusted itself to its unholy spouse as pleasantly as possible.

During these declining years Senior Elder Bell appeared less and less often at the San Francisco Seminary capitol, and it seemed that he had lost interest in his California model of the Universal Service Corporation. However, on December 21, 1951, emerging once again in his earlier cultic role of "The Speaker" for Mankind United, he explained his absence in a startling mimeographed bulletin circulated among his disciples.

Recalling that the Sponsors had promised back in 1939 to place "enough power in the form of inventions and discoveries" into the hands of Mankind United members to release the long-awaited 30-day Program, thus establishing the Universal Service Corporation sometime before December 25, 1951, no matter how unregenerate the outer world remained, "The Speaker" now revealed that the Sponsors had changed their minds. Since, in order to release the world-wide Program, the International Institute of Universal Research and Administration would have to use its secret inventions "to keep hundreds of millions of human beings under the control of suspended animation for an indefinite period of time," the Sponsors had decided that "the overwhelming percentage of lazy, and almost wholly selfish, human beings now occupying this planet" was not worth saving.[24] The cult leader prognosticated:

> Our earth will gradually be abandoned until its evil elements of leadership and population have carried out their self-destruction; and until the poisons released by the widespread use of atom bombs, gasses, and death-rays have ceased to affect life on this earth.[25]

To escape this coming holocaust, "Speaker" Bell and his secret associates in the Research Department of the International Institute had recently explored other planetary systems. Let him elaborate:

> To those who understand, many planets may also be seen to exist where others see but one.

> There exist very nearly identical planetary systems to the one in which our world is located, and seemingly at virtually the same place in the universe. . . . .

> An "infinite" number of objects or ideas may be in the same place at the same time as long as they are each subject to, and respond to, a distinctly different set of so-called natural laws.

> Therefore, all that the Institute's Research scientists had to discover in order to enter an entirely separate planetary system was not how to abridge vast distances, as we usually think of distance, but only how to tune a person out of subjection to

the so-called natural laws of this planetary system and into one subject to an entirely different set of so-called natural laws.[26]

Further divulging the Mankind United discovery, Bell stated,

There seems (after some years of close research) to be but little difference in the outward appearance of the flora and fauna on the planet corresponding to our earth than that which we have right here—except that no evidence of disease can be found.

The Institute's colonists report a very slight native population. . . . The natives of said planet have no objection to the populations of other co-existing planetary systems occupying their world with them. . . .[27]

Describing these "natives," Bell asserted,

Turning back the hand of time and removing any signs of age is no more difficult to them than changing their clothes.

With no other means than the use of thought, they can communicate with one another, irrespective of distance or so-called material barriers. And thought also takes them wherever they wish to go throughout their planetary system, and builds practically everything they wish to construct with no apparent in-between mechanical procedures.[28]

In this heavenly realm "ignorance, greed, poverty, disease, brutality, war, decrepitude, old age, and death are wholly unknown." Here was to be the future home of the Universal Service Corporation, where those who remained loyal to the Mankind United vision would be colonized.

For years past "largely automatic equipment" operating in secret laboratories "many miles below the surface of the earth, and beyond detection," had been "determining the actual thoughts and motives of each person who indicated an interest in the 'Mankind United' Program." Those who survived the "years of exhaustive screening and testing" were to be the pioneer settlers in the other-planetary promised land. The bulletin added,

Our Sponsors will concentrate their principal attention on the operation of the Universal Service Corporation throughout a planetary system previously unheard of and wholly unreachable by the Hidden Rulers.[29]

In recent years, under orders from the Sponsors, the Vigilantes and their trained helpers in the International Institute of Universal Research and Administration had turned their experiments to finding ways and means of transporting the chosen people in Mankind United "beyond the reach of the moronic, but viciously brutal moral idiots who now seem to dominate mankind's destiny." "The Speaker" disclosed further,

The transition, rejuvenation, and re-embodiment of all persons will be solely under the jurisdiction of our Sponsors' Research Department. . . . Those who in their thoughts desire to have this experience, and have shown their right to receive it, will be so classified. Their rate of vibration and the specific nature of their atomic structure (together with certain completely distinct elements of individuality) will be recorded on the largely automatic equipment which brings to pass the desired transition.[30]

Then this equipment, by making a "minutely small change in one's so-called vibrational rate and atomic structure," will bring about their translation to the other-planetary life.

Unfortunately, at the 1951 stage of Mankind United research, the automatic subterranean machinery was able to bring about this translation only "during the brief instant immediately preceding one's so-called death." The Prophetic message continued,

You will awaken with a new, healthy consciousness and a healthy and perfectly formed body. . . . At the very moment that those who believe in your death are arranging to dispose of the body you have abandoned, you will be fully aware of your re-embodiment, rejuvenation, and transition into the kind of life and world envisioned by Christ Jesus.[31]

In concluding his astounding revelation, "Speaker" Bell told his remaining fellow crusaders that their last-moment rebirth into this heavenly utopia depended on their continuing demonstration of the "completely practical teachings of economic equality and the Golden Rule," here and now, on their church projects. "You will thus be more fully prepared to take your place in the new civilization which is your ultimate re-'birthright.'" [32]

Further dimming the waning star of Mankind United—at least for this world—was the disclosure in this bulletin that the Sponsors had pressed their former Division Superintendent into "greatly intensified responsibilities" in his work with the International Legion of Vigilantes, and as a consequence, he could no longer reign over his West Coast Kingdom. In making his exodus from Christ's Church of the Golden Rule, Bell passed his mantle of "Senior Elder" onto the shoulders of one of his most trusted lieutenants, Mrs. Adelaide P. Nordskott, and thereupon vanished from the cult scene.

Left to itself, the venture into utopia languished. Some of the surviving elderly members withdrew in order to become eligible for old-age pensions. Others found their way back into the folds of sympathetic relatives and friends. Of the younger cultists, most forsook Mankind United for jobs in the booming, postwar California economy, only a few of the most zealous remaining loyal.

By mid-1953 the forces of Mankind United had shrunk to a mere 250 followers, mostly in the San Francisco Bay area. Before another year elapsed, a further retreat occurred. Senior Elder Nordskott, beset by an army of creditors, announced the evacuation of the sprawling cult capitol, the San Francisco Seminary Project, and put the building up for sale in order to keep the cult solvent. By 1955 the largest single remaining project was the American Laundry in San Jose with fifty Student Ministers. At this time twenty cultists migrated eastward to a cabin camp-restaurant church project near Denver, Colorado. A dozen others operated a motel project in Napa, California. Of the remaining sixty-five loyal members, most were elderly, working for a bare livelihood on five farm projects scattered throughout northern California. During the next year the cult kingdom continued to disintegrate until in 1956 fewer than a hundred persisted along its arcane way.

This dwindling remnant of would-be uniters of mankind, admitting defeat of their world-saving mission, lived their version of "one for all and all for one," going about their humble tasks, writing their sermon digests, reading their cult literature, placidly awaiting the final day when they were to be rejuvenated and translated to another planetary system—to dwell forever in the Universal Service Corporation of "Mankind—at last—United."

The inhabitants of the planet Earth had disdained to listen. They were beyond redemption. The world was doomed. In the end the Hidden Rulers had triumphed. Earthly mankind remained disunited.

Chapter IV: *"The Voice of the Right Idea"*

PRO: *If the gestapo keyhole peepers, gossip-mongers, busybodies, bureaucratic politicians, and business people who spend their time criticizing, ridiculing and slandering the Division Superintendent . . . had been willing as has he to give up their businesses, their entire personal resources, and eighteen to twenty-two hours per day of their time—literally their entire personal lives—in an attempt to awaken the people of the world in time to have prevented this war, there would have been no war, no slaughtered millions—no tens of millions of men, women and little children in every corner of this world whose hopes and dreams have been destroyed—whose lives have been crushed by the brutal death of their loved ones.**

CON: *Now I look at it this way, that when charges are directly made, as they were made in this case, that the statements of Mankind United are false, Mr. Bell simply can not stand mute. He simply can not say, "All right, prove it." . . . . The burden is on him to come forward and prove that these vital assertions that*

* *Department "A" Bulletin* (Mankind United Publication, July 4, 1944), p. 7.

were made in Mankind United are true. In the absence of the proof of the truth of the statement that there was an organization behind Mankind United or at least an attempt to prove the truth if for some reason it could not be proved in its entirety—I say, in the absence of proof or at least some attempt to prove it, the Court must conclude and does conclude that there were no Sponsors in this movement; that there was no organization; and that the movement was and is Mr. Bell.**

It is meet to call Arthur L. Bell the "Prophet" of Mankind United. He represented himself as a vessel of divine purpose and inspiration; he went among his people and spoke to them; he told them about the genesis of Mankind United; he furnished them with a sacred text; he revealed the "Universal Laws of God"; he offered them the Keys to the Kingdom; he commanded and they responded. Like many a prophet before him, he proved himself in the eyes of his followers; he created a cult goal and tackled the task of bringing it about; he demanded obedience and a world-wide following by virtue of his mission. Many thousand Californians recognized him and his revelation; they did not elect him, he elected himself. Their will was passive before his personal magnetism, metaphysical teachings, occult abilities, and power of office. Truly, he was the indispensable man in the stormy career of the cult.

* Judge Benno M. Brink speaking. *In the Matter of Christ's Church of the Golden Rule, Inc., Bankrupt. In the District Court of the United States for the Southern District of California, Central Division. Reporter's Transcript of proceedings of August 8, 1946*, pp. 29-30.

As we have mentioned earlier, the star in our drama had many stage names. In addition to his official titles, such as the "Division Superintendent," "The Speaker," "The Voice," "Dept. 'A,'" "The Voice of the Right Idea," and the "Church Trustee," Arthur L. Bell at various times took for himself numerous other aliases, e.g., "J. J. Jackson," "L. Patrick," "J. B. Fontaine," "L. Osborne" (under which name he copyrighted the book, *Mankind United*), "Patrick Chapman," etc. In fact, he claimed to have used over 200 aliases, not to deceive but to protect himself and his co-workers from attack and destruction by the Forces of Evil. During the first seven years of the cult drama, while he played his role of Division Superintendent, his name never was used in introducing him at cult meetings. Often he was simply referred to as the "D.S." He derived much of his authority from his official position, unquestioningly accepted by his followers, who thought he was merely one among many Division Superintendents throughout the world. He avoided intimacies or close friendships, even with his immediate subordinates, most of whom first knew him as "J. J. Jackson." Generally his followers viewed him as a mysterious figure, far in the background, and yet occasionally appearing among them in person, to whom they owed and gave unquestioning obedience, and whose name they were to avoid mentioning or referring to in public. Throughout his prophetic career Bell maintained, "I don't permit my name to be used. Newspapers may have used it, but we wanted no personality worship or personality leadership." [1] His followers seconded him, "We serve as channels for Mankind United ideas and ideals . . . as persons we are nothing." [2] This initial difficulty with our Prophet's name is merely the beginning of our struggle against the obscurantism surrounding the man.

Nevertheless, we will have to settle on some real name, and

probably our most accurate solution to the mystery is "Arthur Lowber Osborne Bell," the name he testified to in the later bankruptcy case involving the cult. He was born in Newington, New Hampshire, on March 29, 1900. "My people were in New England many generations," he related. "My father was a Presbyterian minister, my mother, a 'home missionary' and a minister's daughter. . . . I know all about the way the 'orthodox' denominations work. . . . I was orphaned at the age of four. From that time on I had a precarious existence with my mother, helping her to support the family."[3] Dept. "A" further informs us, "The fact that our Pacific Coast Division Superintendent was obliged to largely support himself as a child—and to assist in the support of others while he was still a boy—vividly impressed upon his thought the cruel inequalities and injustice of the world's 'survival of the fittest' (dog-eat-dog) economic system."[4]

Mr. Bell usually was reticent about talking of his background. On one subject, however, he expostulated freely, viz., that "he had come up the 'hard way,' that he was a self-made man," and that whatever he knew, he had "picked up by himself."[5] Indeed, he prided himself in his lack of formal training, openly attesting that he had only four years of "schooling."[6] Apparently early in life he decided to go west to seek his fortune. Relatives living in San Francisco gave him a place to go, and there he went. About this time too, he first came in contact with Christian Science. "I was fifteen," he recounted. "My aunt, who because of it was reviled by the rest of the family, was a Christian Scientist. She introduced me to it. There I found my thirst for truth satisfied. I read *Science and Health and the Key to the Scriptures.* At first I didn't understand it, but I realized that here was something that worked. I joined the Mother Church."[7]

Then World War I came. Near its end he served briefly in the California Coast Artillery and was honorably discharged.

Meanwhile his interest in Christian Science had deepened, and shortly after his release, he decided to become a practitioner. Sketching his life, Dept. "A" reported that "from the time he was seventeen years of age, there was never a day that he could not have lived in luxury and comparative ease had he so desired, for he had the faculty for making money—and in large amounts." [8] Then came 1919, the year the Sponsors took the first steps to accomplish the goals of Mankind United. They did not forget young Bell and allegedly took him into their select International Legion of Vigilantes for the fifteen-year part-time course of instruction.

During this period of his youth there circulated two very popular books describing a utopia strikingly similar to the Universal Service Corporation of Mankind United. These books were *Looking Backward* and its sequel, *Equality,* both by Edward Bellamy, who, according to cult gossip, had been one of the original Sponsors of Mankind United. They deeply impressed Bell. Later he opined that Christian Science was all right, but it failed to go far enough: it adapted itself too complacently to our oppressive system. Bellamy had the right idea. To discover further answers, Bell wandered outside the boundaries of Christian Science. When questioned about his theological training at a State hearing, he replied that his studies had been carried on over many years, "Primarily the Bible . . . books on Christian Science, John Stockings' writings . . . Oh, so many books over the years I don't care to list them. . . ." [9]

During the turbulent twenties California had just begun to sprout. Its tourist trade germinated into big business. Hollywood had begun to spread its shadow over the nearby Californians. The great western migration was on; California was its apex. And Arthur L. Bell thrived amidst the lush business opportunities of the Bay area. His inherent abilities pointed him toward insurance and real estate, and in those boom years of land specu- lation, he prospered. We are told that he "owned and controlled business interests valued at hundreds of thousands of dollars" during this period, but because of the fact that "he considered his business activities as being intended to aid underprivileged people—and that the financial obligations which it was neces- sary to assume for such developments should first be paid— caused him to live as frugally during most of these many years as he would have had he been virtually a pauper." [10] When the depression struck, it hit him hard. But "in spite of a depression that had been very costly to him as well as to others," [11] he claimed that he salvaged the bulk of his worldly fortune.

Mr. Bell was not a celibate prophet. He first wed in 1921, but, according to him, his undercover activities in the Inter- national Legion of Vigilantes, which were secret even to his wife, produced incompatibilities that brought the marriage to the divorce courts in 1931.[12] He remarried in January, 1934, as he told his followers, "only a short time before I was asked to present our Program to the public on the Pacific Coast." [13] His second wife was twenty-nine years his senior and financially well- to-do. Like her husband, she was a Christian Science practitioner, "with the many responsibilities it entails," and since she was absorbed in her work, we are told, she was not able to join her husband's movement.

The Prophet never knew he would receive the "call," but it finally came. Dept. "A" tells us that "less than one year after he married he was called upon to fulfil the pledge he had made to our Sponsors some fifteen years before. . . ." [14] One day he enlivened the court proceedings by testifying that he had received his mantle of office while traveling on a Pullman between Los Angeles and San Francisco. Sleeping in his berth, he had been awakened by a voice that bade him deliver his first lecture. He did not see the speaker but only heard him in the dark.[15] The newly appointed Division Superintendent added that he immediately dedicated his whole being to his task, devoting a prodigious number of hours per week to promulgating the Mankind United idealism. Like the Sponsors, in his official capacity he was never allowed "to personally use any of the funds belonging to, or made available by, Mankind United co-workers." [16]

Meanwhile, because he had no time to manage or liquidate his properties, it was disclosed that "for five years, he watched his personal business interests and plans fall apart and disintegrate before his very eyes (while he carried forward his part in our program). . . . losses which required only the use of his time to prevent." [17] Hence, it was through his wife, he explained, that he had been able to carry on his prophetic ministry. With her independent means and income she had been the "homemaker," completely supporting him, and she had "gladly and generously met the full expense thereof. . . ." [18]

Undoubtedly one of his greatest early problems was to find ways and means of contacting persons who might develop an interest in the message contained in the "bible" that he had just had copyrighted and printed. In addition to his immediate friends he availed himself of the extensive contacts made in his insurance and real estate activities. He ferreted out lists of prospects in many sundry places. An Oakland, California accordion teacher, Mr. Orlando Meniketti, told the Tenney Legislative Fact-Finding Committee that sometime in 1934 Mr. Bell had taken accordion lessons, piano lessons, voice lessons, and dancing lessons in his studio, and that during this time Bell had harried him for lists of his students, their names and addresses, occupations, and approximate incomes. The emerging Prophet surrounded himself with a dreamy air of obscurity and mystery, causing Mr. Meniketti to recall that Bell once told him of a race of men with metallic heads, very large to indicate their mental development, "located some place, and I believe it was underground; and he said they controlled all our earthquakes and were responsible for that and floods and things of that kind, you see? . . . He was the type of man who was always the same, who had a complacent attitude, always smiling and good-natured . . . he mentioned to me, at one time, that after he got this movement started I would never see him again; but I'd hear his voice. . . . He told me of his journeys in his sleep. . . . I didn't know what to make out of him; I was always mystified by him." [19] Shortly after being refused the list, Mr. Bell dropped the lessons.

The Division Superintendent gave all credit to the Sponsors for his mysterious occult powers, which took numerous forms. One of the most widely believed stories concerned his "doubles." According to attorneys for the State of California, Mr. Bell claimed to be assisted in his duties by "seven persons who appear, act, talk, and think precisely as he does and who thus enable him to do the work of eight men and to be in practical effect in many different places at the same time." [20] On one occasion he informed the Tenney Committee that his doubles lived in different parts of the country. "They were appointed and given to me as assistants . . . I do not know their real names. . . . Occasionally they make speeches for me. . . . Often 'doubles' would make payments for me. . . . The use of 'doubles' is solely one of convenience, not of deception—to save time. I still have to work twenty to twenty-two hours per day." [21]

The story of the doubles circulated largely by word of mouth among the different local units of the group. For instance, in December, 1942, "The Speaker" revealed how his doubles confounded the Hidden Rulers and their dupes, who "would hand quite a few million dollars to anyone who would get two of us together at the same time, and let their plastic surgeons try to figure out how we do it, even to duplicating finger prints. . . . We are not going to satisfy their curiosity." Upon another occasion he told his listeners, "Often I am in charge of three or four meetings at one time." A former cult adherent stoutly maintained that at a huge Mankind United meeting held at the Shrine auditorium in Los Angeles in June, 1939, she sat in the first row and was sure that she saw one of the doubles peek in from the wings. Afterward, although violently critical of the Prophet, she still believed that he had doubles. Another woman, for years one of his most loyal disciples, recalled, "He once made me buy seven ties, all alike, for his doubles. Another time, while talking to me over the phone, he said that he had one of his doubles beside him and that he was going to put him on, to see if their voices sounded alike. I couldn't tell much difference." Naturally rumors snowballed and added zest to cult gossip. Belief in the doubles was virtually unanimous, but the question was "How was it done?" The more faithful felt it was something beyond human knowledge; the more skeptical conjectured, "You know all the ways of 'making-up' in the movies. Why couldn't they use the same?"

During one of his numerous appearances before the Tenney Legislative Committee, "The Voice of the Right Idea," speaking with his usual cocksureness, elucidated his powers of translevitation (i.e., ability to transport himself to any place in an instant). Again crediting the Sponsors, he told how they had dispatched him to all the major nations of the world, including several trips to China, but he disclaimed knowing the method they had employed. "I am quite sure they didn't use the airlines, ships, or trains," he glibly told the legislators, "It's not quite physical, but I never noticed any body changes. . . . I was used as a mail carrier, transporting records, documents, or instructions. . . . I was told to be at a certain point at a certain time—I went to sleep—later awakened at a distant locality. Received instruction, went to sleep again—found myself at my destination." [22] He received his extraordinary power only for official Mankind United business. "I delivered records into the hands of messengers, the identity of the personality of whom I am not familiar." [23]

"The Voice" added another fillip to the hearing by recounting that just before the beginning of World War II, the day before Germany attacked Poland, he was attending to his official duties in San Francisco when suddenly he found himself in the middle of the Atlantic Ocean on board the steamer, *The City of Richmond*. Then somehow, beyond his senses, he received information that war was to be declared the following day. He informed the ship's officers of the exact time and place and how it would happen. His rejoinder to the nonbelieving legislators was that they could check with the ship's officers.

Speaking at one of the cult auditoriums, "The Voice" revealed to his followers that he "could go through a wall if he wanted to," adding that he often left the auditorium "through the roof of the building." [24] He then went into a deep metaphysical discourse on the infinite powers of the mind when accompanied by faith. His listeners had heard tales of the power of the great Indian mystics. One of them, a "Sister Ala," had actually served for a time as a Bureau Manager. They considered it eminently possible that their leader had access to the occult wisdom of the ages and consequently could dissociate his mind from his body. In fact, some claimed this power, to a lesser degree, themselves. They felt that Mr. Bell, in order to accomplish a complete translevitation, would have to penetrate into the upper aeons of pure metaphysics, but "he was a wonderful metaphysician."

"The Voice" of Mankind United, once he had been exposed to public view, became prize copy for news reporters, especially those writing for the many sensation-peddling newspapers on the California scene. He at once became their favorite prototype, almost too good to be true, of an extremist cult leader. In their lead sentences they variously described him as "fabulous and magnetic," "tall, dark, and handsome," "a tall man with dark eyes, long sideburns, and flashing eyes," "profit's prophet," etc.; and indeed he did boast more than a voice. Physically he was impressive, not in the traditional saintly way, but in the more modern sense of the go-getting, hard-driving businessman. He stood about five feet ten inches and weighed in the neighborhood of 180 pounds. Although he had a well-fed look, he was not noticeably obese. His black, bushy head of hair and his long sideburns were just beginning to turn gray. Shadowing his eyes were massive eyebrows, usually trimmed, that joined above the nose. His dark gray eyes drooped somewhat, but they were clear and shrewd. Their pupils constantly shifted and stared, causing some of his onetime intimates to attest to their hypnotic quality. Normally, they were not warm; when Mr. Bell was angry, they became ice-cold, and then, too, his mouth assumed a derisive curl. His nose was domineering and well shaped;

his lips, full and firm; his forehead, high. By and large, he presented a handsome appearance. Little wonder one acute observer called him the "John Barrymore of the California cults."

He was the kind of man that elderly women admire and dote over, middle-aged women secretly love, and young women adulate. Numerous feminine ex-followers vouched that such-and-such a loyal woman co-worker was "in love" with Mr. Bell. He had a charming way with the weaker sex. After court sessions he always turned to converse smilingly and affably with his feminine constituents. He gave them attention, and simultaneously he ordered them about. They responded with pleasure. However, he failed to evince a similar masculine appeal: perhaps it was the expensive musk that he used, which lent him an exotic, quasi-oriental air.

He espoused teetotalism, claiming to be a non-drinker, non-smoker, and a vegetarian. It is true that, although he did not require it, he encouraged his followers to refrain from eating meat or meat products. Numerous headwaiters in Pacific Coast hotels knew him as "Mr. J. J. Jackson" and carried his favorite salad dressing. His lavish tips helped them to remember.

Shortly after Division Superintendent Bell was arrested as a violator of the Wartime Sedition Act in December, 1942, stories began to appear in the newspapers regarding his habit of frequenting various swank night clubs. He took these "slanderous" rumors so seriously that he felt obliged to counter them, explaining that the Research Department of the International Institute had ordered him to investigate the "degeneration of the moral fibre of the community." "Part of my responsibilities consists of periodically gathering information on the glorified, plush-lined pig-pens known as cocktail parlors," he disclosed to a conclave of subofficials, adding, "I had never seen the inside of a night

club until it was known that our mail was being tampered with.
. . . In the last three or four years, however, we have developed
a very smooth-running system of memo and mail delivery through
such channels." Anticipating further sensational stories, he
warned them:

> A great deal is going to be said about your Division Superin-
> tendent . . . that "slippery person—the most slippery individual
> in the United States"—and his way of living. If they dared to
> bring it out in their trial, they could prove that I have appeared in
> seven or eight different night clubs in seven or eight different
> cities on the same night and at the same time . . . but that might
> confirm my claim to having a number of doubles—which would
> greatly weaken and confuse their case. . . .
> As to how much or how little wine I (or my doubles) may
> have imbibed—in acting the part we have to act—it is not im-
> portant. We shall not lower ourselves to answer gossip or types
> of slanderous attack unless there is something to be gained by our
> answering them.[25]

Mr. Bell lived well. He dressed immaculately. He fre-
quented only the best hotels and restaurants. Although he continually flitted about his cult empire, he never actually lived
among his disciples on any of the cult projects. He once told his
followers that for purposes of privacy and for the best interests
of those who trusted him with the responsibilities he had to assume, it was essential for him to occupy a certain type of home
environment. Concretely, this home environment consisted of
several fashionable apartments in Los Angeles and San Francisco,
and several luxurious mansions in Burlingame and West Hollywood. Needless to say, the Los Angeles press licked its chops
when, during a raid on one of these, a $75,000 mansion overlook-
ing Hollywood's Sunset Strip, State agents discovered amazingly
sumptuous furnishings including a swimming pool, a sixty-foot

living room containing a pipe organ, oriental-draped love seats, and opening behind a billiard rack, a secret cocktail bar fitted with a trick air jet in the floor like those found in amusement park fun houses. One State investigator estimated $50,000 to be the minimum amount spent for the maintenance and living expenses of Bell between 1938 and 1945, an amount his wife contributed to his ministry. Since he had no income, he paid no income tax, a fact inciting no little interest among State and Federal tax officials.

This flair for the good life lent the Division Superintendent an imposing presence when he appeared as the featured speaker at a typical mass meeting during the heyday of Mankind United. After being given a somewhat obsequious introduction, he strolled with a rolling gait onto the speaker's rostrum. He wore a finely tailored, double-breasted blue suit, topped off by an expensive silk, splash-figured tie, which incidentally, after he had assumed his later role of Church Trustee, became dark and conservative, as a Christian minister's should be. Reaching the rostrum, he paused, calmly closed the lower button of his coat while smilingly and intently surveying the audience, and then began his talk.

The appellation, "The Voice," was no misnomer. He spoke in a low, well-modulated tone that immediately brought his listeners to attention and made them expectant of what was to come. "Here is a man in high position in our organization," they thought, "who speaks as one who has authority, who is used to commanding." It was an unctuous voice, betraying a pompous but not blatant affection. It was a voice that maintained itself when consciously attended to. Sometimes his followers had to strain to catch his words, at other times it swelled throughout the auditorium. There was a lucid, personal note in it. He purred; he inflected; he used many illustrations. His gestures were relaxed and excellently executed. He never read his lectures. His eyes kept roaming over his audience, adding contact to his words. He adopted an aloof, superior mien, as one cognizant of his position and power, yet somehow every listener felt that his leader was speaking to him or her personally, just as though only the two of them were conversing on the subject.

All the cult followers, even those who became embittered and dropped out, attested to this magnetic quality in the Prophet. Said one, "He was able to hold an audience spellbound." Another recalled having been "thrilled and entranced" for six hours listening to him one night, adding, "He made goose-pimples run up my back. I had never heard anybody like him and I've heard a lot of 'science' lectures." Several opined that "it was a kind of mass hypnotism, or maybe telepathy." One woman, formerly one of his most enthusiastic supporters, related, "I've heard many talks on metaphysics and economics before, but he made them much more plausible and clear. Even after you went home, the talk still looked good—even days afterwards it thrilled you." [26] These were typical responses.

Such an impact was not always accidental. In planning large mass meetings Division Superintendent Bell sometimes cleverly set the stage for his appearance. By pre-arrangement, he purposely delayed his arrival at the auditorium until everyone inside had been reseated alphabetically, and throughout the reseating, underlings carefully ferreted about, looking for dictaphones. For perhaps an hour after the scheduled starting time, the cultists waited expectantly, while the tension mounted. Then the rear doors burst open, the Division Superintendent bustled briskly up the aisle followed by several scampering aides, and after being introduced, apologized for being late—the pressure of his duties, etc.

In talking to smaller cult groups, "The Voice" often interjected homey colloquialisms, such as "by golly," or "by jimminy." His disciples relished this habit. While they were never allowed to forget their crucial misson on which depended the very fate of civilization, still, they were basically simple folk. When their leader talked to them in their language, they felt a strengthening of their spiritual bond to him.

But on the whole, he failed to get down to concrete particulars in describing his grandiose program. There were vaguenesses and generalities, usually projected into sizes of six figures, in most of his talks. Here was a typical rejoinder, "I defy any statistician to refute my claim that in ten years the world could produce an ample supply of food to last a hundred years, and they have natural refrigerators at the North and South poles." [27]

He wove the message of Mankind United into a mellifluous melody of many parts including New Testament quotations, metaphysical laws, economic utopianism, and last but not least, appeals for money. Early in life, as an insurance salesman, he had learned the basic tenet of advertising that "there is no substitute for a good label." Bell had a talent for coining appealing names. "Mankind United" was a stroke of genius; similarly, the other appellations he attached to the various institutes, bureaus, and offices of his cult. They fitted in well with the metaphysics. There was the connotation of "Universality," "Brotherhood," and the "Golden Rule," combined with "science," "research," "progress," and the "Golden Age." In using these terms he cleverly associated ideas already heavily and favorably weighted in the minds of his followers, who tended to lump them all together.

Like many other autodidacts, he occasionally manifested a subtle hostility toward higher learning, upon one occasion stating bluntly, "All theology to me is something that should have been dead and buried centuries ago." [28] His style of writing was another yardstick of his education. He often used carelessly split infinitives; he habitually wrote in long, periphrastic, abstract sentences; yet, he had an excellent command of simple metaphors, interspersing them throughout his lectures and writings. Many of them were timeworn, even dead, but others were fresh and fitted well into the context of what he said.

He felt that if an idea was worth saying once, it was worth saying two or three times, consequently, his speeches often sounded exceedingly redundant. His stock in religious trade was always on display, ready for immediate use. It was common for him to exhort his followers to read a certain piece of cult literature again and again, even twenty or thirty times, until it was part of their unconscious thinking. Seemingly he followed the same practice; he believed repetition was the most efficacious means of learning a worthwhile truth. Be that as it may, his followers equated his style with profundity and imitated it in their own writing and speech. He put into words what they felt and believed, and in so doing, he was automatically vested with a measure of the attraction that the ideals and principles of Mankind United enjoyed.

For ostensibly these ideals and principles constituted the only leadership to which the cultists paid homage. Above all else, Mankind United claimed to be a rational association. The officials, from the Division Superintendent down, were merely the impersonal channels through which the cult doctrine was broadcast to the world. The revelations of the Prophet, whether his lectures, his mimeographed tracts, or the textbook, enjoyed the prestige of the secret Mankind United hierarchy for which he was "The Speaker." Similarly his commands were lent validity. Now the wile of the cult myth becomes apparent. If most Mankind Uniters had been asked to believe that Arthur L. Bell personally was the source of the cult doctrine and the many categorical orders that accompanied his revelations, they would have had little disposition to join his one-man crusade. But given their supreme belief in a powerful, world-wide organization behind him, his cult success was assured.

Even his most bitter adversaries testified to the unusual personality and appearance of "The Voice" of Mankind United. Everyone who knew him respected his abilities as a cult leader. Some feared that he might grow into a West Coast "Huey Long" and that his cult organization might prove a success and sprout throughout the country. However, during the declining career of the cult covering the six-year period of bankruptcy proceedings, he was kept suspended like a ping-pong ball bouncing atop two or three jets of water, never falling to the ground. Unable to unburden himself of this litigation, he was diverted from peddling his bill of goods on the California cult market.

By late 1951 his prophetic zeal had burned out. In abandoning his West Coast model of the Universal Service Corporation for the nether laboratories of the International Institute of Universal Research and Administration, "The Voice of the Right Idea," after describing his interplanetary explorations, left his disciples with these words:

I deeply hope that this will not prove to be my farewell message on this planet to you who have been my close associates and greatly loved fellow-crusaders these past many years; but should it not be possible or wise for me to send further bulletins to you, I ask that you turn to the all-knowing Mind that is God for wisdom to understand and abide by the all-important truths contained herein. ALL OF ME THAT IS OF VALUE TO OTHERS HAS BEEN GIVEN TO YOU IN THE CONCEPTS EXPRESSED IN MY WRITINGS AND SERMONS. THESE I BEQUEATH TO MANKIND WITH SAID BEQUEST TO BE ADMINISTERED SOLELY BY THE ECCLESIASTICAL SOCIETY OF CHRIST'S CHURCH OF THE GOLDEN RULE. . . .[29]

And his swan song was ultimately hopeful:

KEEP YOUR FAITH AND YOUR VISION BRIGHT AND CLEAR FOR ALMOST BEFORE YOU KNOW THAT IT HAS HAPPENED, YOU WILL HAVE PASSED THROUGH THE MISTS OF UNCERTAINTY AND CONFUSION OF THOUGHT AND WILL BE LIVING AS GOD INTENDED THAT HIS CHILDREN SHOULD LIVE.[30]

Chapter V: *Uniter of Mankind*

> Follow your favorite group just so long as it moves toward unity of all the multitude of *New Race* groups in America.*

Cultic Vistas

In the heart of downtown Los Angeles is the Embassy Hotel, containing a large auditorium and numerous smaller halls. Over the course of the past thirty-five years this building has become a favorite center of operations for Southern California cults. Every night usually two of three groups congregate to make the halls reverberate with matters occult, astrological, utopian, and metaphysical. Scrutiny of these audiences reveals a rather homogeneous lot, physically not unlike any cross section of Southern California inhabitants. However, there is a verve to their talk and a disturbing light in their eyes. They want something; they believe they have found what they want; and they are almost fanatically determined to achieve what they want. Observing them in action forces the conclusion, although the evidence is circumstantial, that here is a simmering emotional volcano that might erupt at any time into a new religious movement. And if Carey McWilliams is right in predicating that "What America is, California is, with accents, in italics," [1] it would be unrealistic to assume that this is an eccentric tendency to be found only in the Southern California country.

The habitué of this constellation of cults, whom we shall

---

* *MYSTIC AMERICA* (anonymous, non-Mankind United tract, n.d.).

call the *cult individual,* is the subject of the ensuing chapter. We have focused, of course, upon the adherents to Mankind United, but the term, cult individual, refers not to the average cultist but to an ideal type, an extreme picture of the all-out cult devotee drawn from many individual cases. It is an image of the general cult personality distilled from many different persons, their histories, their views, and their goals.*

The cult individual is at home not only in Mankind United. His intellect is eclectic; he is willing to avail himself of truths and facts from any source. Characteristically, he prides himself in his freedom from bigotry. His aim, he will tell you, is to obtain the truth, and whatever group or groups offer him the maximum satisfaction in his quest for wisdom, he will study and follow. Accordingly, in addition to Mankind United, he knows something about the Lemurians, the Rosicrucians, the Technocrats, the Mormons, the Anglo-Israelites, "I AM," New Thought, Unity, Theosophy, Yoga, Hermetics, Mentalphysics, pyramidology, spiritualism, the Oahspe Bible, faith-healing, flying saucers and the latest metaphysical innovations. He has served his term in the Townsend Plan and the "Ham and Eggs" scheme. Much of this cult information leaves him indifferent; yet, selecting what seem to him to be pertinent tidbits of knowledge, he adds them to his stock of cultic convictions.

In most cases the cult individual engages in the activities of several or more cult groups. Ordinarily this division of labor is acceptable to the respective prophets, some of whom admit that there are truths elsewhere. It was only when Mankind United entered its Christ's Church form that membership in other groups had to be relinquished. In the over-all cult world a person might simultaneously belong to the Technocrats and the Rosicrucians;

* See Appendix A for further analysis of the term.

he might attend Flying Saucer Conventions in Hollywood hotels; in the meantime he might maintain his membership in the Mother Church of Christian Science while becoming familiar with stellar healing, induced emotion, and extrasensory perception at the Religion of the Stars services.

To him horizons are unlimited! He propounds that no single group has a monopoly on truth. In fact, at one time many cultists delighted in making veiled assertions that these different groups were secretly interconnected, only awaiting the opportune moment to unite and demonstrate their verities to a benighted world. It was rumored that in the not-too-distant future these groups will emerge as powerful forces in society, even as the prophesied "sixth race." There was great disappointment in 1951 when the Aquarian Age was ushered in without these prophecies being fulfilled.

Hence, it is palpable that when we look for the cult type of person, we may find him under many different banners, yet his kind is fundamentally homogeneous. No specific Mankind United nor Lemurian nor "I AM" species exist. The cult individual is a more generic type. However, within the boundaries of Mankind United there is the material to sculpture him in clear-cut relief.[*]

Vital Statistics

Secret orders . . . zombie-like silence . . . strict and unquestioning obedience to the will of a master . . . humble subservience of self to a fantastic dream of a world-wide cooperative tagged "Universal Service Corporation". . . .[**]

[*] See Appendix D for intimate case histories of several Uniters of Mankind.
[**] *Los Angeles Herald Express* (November 5, 1945), p. 1.

Ever on the lookout for the bizarre, newspaper and magazine writers have created a stereotype of the California cultist that depicts him as a "zany crackpot," a deluded and benighted person bordering on lunacy. Readers almost come to expect him to be an extremist physically as well as intellectually, literally a race apart. Perhaps the ensuing description will serve to deflate this stereotype, at least in part, and show the cultist as he really is, not so very different, in terms of vital statistics, from the average son and daughter of the Golden West.

Racially the Mankind United follower descended from northwestern European stock. His surname indicated forebears predominantly from England, Scandinavia, Germany, and Ireland, along with a few from Italy and France. If any Mexicans, Negroes, Orientals, or Jews appeared among the converts, they were the exception rather than the rule. Ostensibly they were welcome, however, for the Mankind United creed vigorously denounced all intolerance—whether of another race, religion, or occupation.

Neither was he a newcomer to the State. A sample of forty-four cultists revealed an average period of residence in California of 24.4 years, a fact indicating that, although most of them were not natives, nevertheless they had resided there most of their adult life. And they were about average in their mobility: some had confined themselves to a single California community all their lives; others had moved frequently, as the convenience of their employment required. As a whole, in this respect they were no more unstable than their fellow Californians.

As for their place of birth: here too the cult members failed to differ from the other inhabitants of the region. Some were native sons; some were southerners; a large percentage was from the Midwest; a number were easterners; and finally, a few were born in various European countries (of these practically all had become United States citizens).

Although the converts to Mankind United ranged in age from sixteen to eighty-four, most likely they were middle-aged. To assume that the cult was simply a haven for the aged and decrepit is erroneous. A sample of 242 members disclosed the following age groupings:

Under 30 years	21
30-39 years	22
40-49 years	70
50-59 years	63
60-69 years	44
Over 70 years	22

Since minors most likely were brought into the cult orbit by their parents, they were not included in the above calculations. Also, the scarcity of proselytes under forty years of age may be explained, at least partially, by the military draft, which during the 1940's drained off the men in the younger age groups.

Contrary to common preconceptions, the cult world was not overrun by the fair sex. A sample of 723 Student Ministers in Christ's Church of the Golden Rule showed 295 men and 428 women, a ratio of not quite three men to four women. The fact that women enjoyed equal rights with men, having an equal opportunity to work their way up in cult ranks, may have been a factor here. After the childbearing stage in their lives, too, their need for meaningful activity may have been greater than that of their working husbands. Regardless of these possibilities, women certainly failed to dominate the movement; most projects, al-

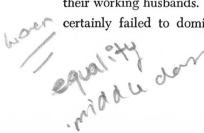

though varying with the type of workers needed, were fairly well divided between men and women.

Almost always the Student Minister had covered a wide gamut of occupations, taking pride in having worked at many different jobs. The cult attracted those from virtually all walks of life, but most were from middle class areas. Since the movement was predominantly an urban rather than a rural phenomenon, most occupations fitted into the urban category. In a sample of 210 of its followers were the following occupational groupings:*

Businessmen	4
Professional men	15
Semiprofessional men	18
White-collar workers	56
Skilled workers	44
Semiskilled workers	64
Unskilled workers	9

Along with these figures go several interesting sidelights. First, there was a generous sprinkling of chiropractors in the cult world, for, though scorned by the outside doctors of medicine, they were given respect and status by the Uniters of Mankind. Also joining up were several ex-Fundamentalist ministers who asserted that they had advanced in understanding to the Mankind United level. Numerous self-styled lecturers saw the cult as an opportune field to cultivate. Both the nursing and teaching pro-

* The "Semiprofessional" classification includes those in borderline professions, such as chiropractic, accountancy, and lecturing. The "White-collar" category includes those working in nonadministrative office or clerical capacities. The "Skilled worker" group includes, among others, artisans, craftsmen, and farmers. The "Semiskilled workers" were mostly factory workers.

fessions provided many proselytes. Since most of the cultists had joined as married couples, probably the most common occupation was that of housewife. There was one type of person who seldom was attracted—that was the shrewd, hard-headed businessman who operated his own establishment. Likewise, no person of great wealth saw an advantage in joining the group.

The average education of the cultists fell into the ninth- or tenth-grade level, but there were extreme cases in both directions. Often the cult convert, forced by personal or family situation, had left school while still in the grades. Especially was this true of those over forty-five. Sometimes superimposed over the public school education was training in trade schools, night schools, and technical schools. A feminine "Ph.D.," when queried about her degree, vaguely explained that it stood for "Doctor of Metaphysical Science." One garrulous Student Minister laid claim to both a Ph.D. and a D.D. Actually, those with the highest formal education were the pharmacists, engineers, schoolteachers, and chiropractors. Conspicuously absent from cult circles was one educated type—the liberal arts graduate of a first-rate college.

Those with the least formal education, perhaps compensating, most strongly emphasized their informal training, valuing it above anything they had learned in school. They usually implied that through years of self-study they had drunk from mainsprings of knowledge that flowed only in cultic pastures outside the walls of schools and colleges. In contrast to the inhabitants of the outer world, who fitted their thinking into the orthodox patterns of churches, schools, or other institutions, the Uniters of Mankind sought more extreme explanations for the manifold problems confronting the world—until, in their informal study, they discovered the textbook issued by the International Registration Bureau of Mankind United.

"WORLD-SAVERS WANTED!!!"

A CHALLENGE TO "MAD AMBITION" AND "THE MONEY CHANGERS" ACCOMPANIED BY AN INVITATION TO THE WORLD'S "SANE" MEN AND WOMEN." *

BIGOTED SKEPTICISM AND INEVITABLE EXTERMINATION—OR— INTELLIGENT CO-OPERATION AND "ECONOMIC EQUALITY" . . . WHICH SHALL IT BE? **

CHRISTIANS OF THE WORLD! . . . HAVE YOU THE COURAGE TO ACCEPT OUR INVITATION? ***

"When I read the textbook it answered questions that I had been asking all my life." This confession often marked a milestone in the lifelong search for meaning along which the inquisitive cultist had traveled. He prided himself in the breadth of his experiences, which, he asserted, had been his greatest teacher. He commonly related that his intimate glimpses into hard, cold reality, the world as it really was, had given him insights that ultimately beckoned him into the Mankind United crusade.

His introduction to the crusade came when one of the "World-Savers" who had already joined, usually a relative or friend, showed him the textbook and urged him to read it, at the same time explaining, albeit vaguely, the story of the Sponsors, the International Institute of Universal Research and Administration, the Universal Service Corporation, etc. His friend lent him a copy of the cult bible, and he in turn agreed to read it carefully within three days and then return it to its owner for further lending out. Undoubtedly many readers were indifferent, others were

* Subtitle of the cult textbook, *Mankind United.*
** Title of chapter XVI of *Mankind United.*
*** Title of chapter XIX of *Mankind United.*

dubious, others even suspicious and hostile, but there was a residue that was enthusiastic about its contents, accepting the "Call to Arms" issued by the Sponsors of Mankind United to embark upon "the most glorious adventure ever experienced by the men and women of any age." [2]

To demonstrate his interest, he purchased a personal copy of the book, whereupon he was referred to the Manager of the local Mankind United bureau to be registered. If, for example, he lived in Southern California, shortly thereafter he received an invitation with an aura of mystery about it telling him about a meeting in a downtown Los Angeles auditorium where an urgent and important message was to be delivered by "The Voice of the Right Idea." He awaited the designated night. When he appeared at the door, he was met by a smiling, well-dressed, middle-aged woman who took his invitation and, after a friendly "Good evening," handed him a handbill on which he read, "WE ARE NOT CATTLE!—nor need we be slaughtered merely because of the contempt of our political rulers who consider us as such." [3]

Inside he found the auditorium well filled, even though he arrived fifteen minutes before the proceedings began. There was a friendly intimacy in the air. Probably 500 people sat chatting affably among themselves, yet obviously anticipating what was to take place. Everyone came to attention when the first speaker appeared. After several preliminary talks, largely of a business nature, "The Voice" made his impressive entry onto the stage. His subject for the evening: "The Golden Rule or the Rule of Gold—which shall it be?" After the lecture a mimeographed blank was circulated among those present who "truly desire facts, figures, proofs, and enlightenment." If the visitor signed and returned this form, he was invited to certain future sessions of a more confidential nature. A Bureau Captain shortly called on him to "talk over

persona-to-person devotees

some of the important items which cannot be touched upon in
public meetings." He was called upon to buy more books and to
circulate them among his friends and relatives. If he continued
to react favorably and become more involved, he had taken the
first basic steps toward becoming an active cultist.

The cult prophet dangled numerous appeals before the eyes
of prospective converts. First of all, there was little doubt concerning the class of people toward which he leveled his appeal.
The textbook reverberated with pleas exhorting the *middle class*
to action. Both the French Revolution and the Russian Revolution were cited as examples of uprisings by the "world's most
downtrodden and poverty-stricken 'lower classes.'" Throughout
the centuries the middle classes had been kept much too busy to
take the time to learn what was actually going on in the political
and economic life of their respective countries, hence they had
been mercilessly exploited by politicians and others in the service
of the Hidden Rulers. Now Mankind United proposed to remedy
their situation, issuing a call to arms to the "middle economic
(upper intellectual) class," which comprises the "sanest, the most
industrious, and the most idealistic world group." [4]

"The Voice" of Mankind United also called to his *feminine
listeners,* particularly those of middle age. All the literature, including the textbook, espoused complete women's suffrage: never
were "men" alone referred to, always "men and women." Both
sexes were to share alike in the alluring benefits of the forthcoming Universal Service Corporation. The cult metaphysics proclaimed the "Motherhood" as well as the "Fatherhood" of God.
And then of course many of the fair sex were attracted by the
magnetism of the Prophet's personality. Probably the most inde-
fatigable workers in cultdom were women.

A third major appeal was directed at the *aged.* Here the

cult followed the typical California pattern that such successful ventures as the Townsend Plan, "Ham and Eggs," and the EPIC Movement have exploited. Cult literature posed such questions as "Does the private profit system offer security to 'old people'? Is 'old age' an unescapable penalty of life? . . . What does Mankind United intend to do about 'old people'?" And it answered that under the Universal Service Corporation "elderly citizens . . . will be loved, respected, and cared for. . . ." [5]

But more than simply promising these elderly persons relief, the cult provided a *raison d'etre* to those who felt discarded or unwanted: it made them feel that they mattered as persons and satisfied their desire to do something constructive. They were told that "Old folks need something to live for; something of interest to think about. Well! We have all this and more in Mankind United." [6]

A fourth element, closely related to the appeal to the aged, was the appeal to the *economically insecure*—those able to work but fearful of unemployment and depression. The whole Mankind United plan of salvation aimed to relieve this insecurity. The Sponsors voiced their sense of outrage at the injustices suffered by the "have-nots" at the hands of the "Money Changers." "ARE WE GOING TO REMAIN IN BONDAGE TO A HANDFUL OF 'DEPRAVED MANIACS' WHO THINK THEY HAVE BEEN 'DIVINELY ORDAINED' TO OWN OUR WORLD AND DOMINATE ITS INHABITANTS?" [7] exhorted the textbook. "Each normal man or woman arrives with the same number of hands and feet, but they come with their hands empty and no shoes on their feet, and they leave the same way. They bring no proofs of their superiority with them when they come and they take none with them when they go." [8] With the establishment of the Universal Service Corporation there was to be no opportunity for those who think themselves superior to disturb the welfare of the majority. Then it will be the sons of Beelzebub rather than the sons of men who will have no place to lay their heads.

Practically always the cult follower admitted firsthand, personal contact with the suffering entailed by poverty. It was something he had experienced or seen around him. He had seen elderly men and women standing in block-long bread lines; in fact, he may have stood in one himself. He described families living in sheds because they had no houses. He had offered haven to transients with no place to eat or sleep. He had seen undernourished children clad in rags and ravaged by rickets.

These stark specters of poverty and their concomitant sufferings chilled him. A Student Minister who had previously worked for a consumers' cooperative recalled:

If you had had the experience I had with the cooperatives: it's really too bad to talk about. I've had workers get out stuff that wasn't fit to eat—people on relief were glad to get it. You can't think when you're hungry. Starving is the weapon used by the Hidden Rulers to keep people from thinking. Anybody who has been through what I have sure has to think.[9]

Another typical pattern was that of the feminine adherent who, after finishing the eighth grade, went to work as a clerk in a delicatessen, meanwhile living in boarding houses. Other similar jobs followed in succession, until finally she opened her own restaurant, working as cook. At twenty-three she married a "good man who thought like me." Then the depression struck.

There were times when we didn't know where our next meal was coming from. We had no money in the bank. We couldn't hardly pay rent. Nobody could get a job. There was no work for my husband. No money to buy clothes. Then came the earthquake experience. We were in the middle of it. My but conditions were terrible! That's one of the reasons the economics of

Mankind United appealed to us. We didn't want to see it happen again.[10]

Then there was Henry. Henry homesteaded in Western Canada at the age of twenty-one. He worked hard. Life on this northern frontier was frugal. Just to make a bare living required long hours of labor, often in cold winter weather, but he stayed with it. While on a hunting trip he had his right arm shot off. Another time he was lost in a Canadian blizzard. Then came the depression and the local banks foreclosed. Forced to sell, he received $250 for farm equipment that cost him $7500. "I learned firsthand how the banks work," he explained. "I began to read about them and I soon saw how they control our whole economy." [11] Whereupon Henry, feeling impotent to "buck the money system," pulled up stakes and migrated to a warmer clime. But his reception in Los Angeles was not much warmer. He had to go through many job-hunting experiences, and he asserted that "there is nothing I hate worse than looking for a job. I never could figure out why, when a person could produce in a day many times what he needed to live, yet in our private profit system he could barely make a living." [12] At this time Henry discovered Mankind United and ultimately entered Christ's Church of the Golden Rule. Lifted out of the economic insecurity he had experienced all his life, he ardently dedicated himself to the cult mission, working on a laundry project, loyal to the very end.

These cases were typical of the average cultist. Before joining Mankind United, jarred by worries, fears, and frustrations that seemingly were beyond his control, he no longer felt at home among the accepted institutions of our society; in fact, he actually felt alienated toward it. He lived *in* society but was not *of* it. He seemed oversensitive to the fact that his very livelihood depended upon the whims of an employer, and he directed his consequent resentment toward the system that, he felt, perpetually threatened him. He rationalized the reasons he had failed, and his answers casting blame on the "dog-eat-dog profit system" were substantiated by the textbook. To explain his failure he had merely to point at the Hidden Rulers. According to an ex-follower, "Certain elements in society kept me from developing. . . . The Hidden Rulers, all forces of evil, don't like to see people get ahead. . . . It's a weapon of the Hidden Rulers not to let people get satisfied. People might think." [13]

Within the orbit of the church project the Student Minister no longer was caught in the throes of American competition. One related that, after he went onto a project, it took him some time to accustom himself to the different atmosphere—"There was no pressure." Another loyal follower added with a benign smile,

> When I walk along the streets of San Jose, it's like being in a foreign land among strangers. It's hard to explain. Perhaps it's caused by the evil vibrations of their thoughts. I feel lost and I want to get home to the laundry group. That's one of the important things that the project does . . . it brings "like-minded" people together. "Heaven is simply Harmony." We have harmony here. . . .[14]

Very often the cultist had been a lonely person before joining the movement. Especially was this true if he happened to live in a fast growing, highly mobile urban area where he seldom found neighbors that thought as he did. When Mankind United came along it brought him into contact with his kind of people, ending his isolation and affording him the intimate camaraderie he craved.

Once he crossed the border into the cult world, emotional contagion was the accepted order of things. Here was a lush garden of gossip and augury. Amazing stories circulated privately and openly. Major news events were viewed as omens, meaningful to those who had the Mankind United key to present-day events. Exaggerated rumors on such topics as "This coming Christmas the Sponsors are starting the 30-day Program," "Mr. Bell is actually a reincarnation of Edward Bellamy," and "Within a month the government is going to seize all our property" added fuel to the cultic excitement.

This ominous atmosphere had its effects. The loyal Student Minister oftentimes peered at the outsider with a frightened, intense stare like that of a person suffering from a lack of sleep. News reporters unkindly described him as "zombie-like." His conversation was uniformly guarded. His distrust and fear were obvious, goaded on by recurrent warnings from the cult headquarters. Looking back, a former member recalled, "The frenzy of our enthusiasm made us believe almost anything. We were 'mentally conditioned' by what went on. . . . And most of all we 'mesmerized' ourselves. It took years to create the kind of mental atmosphere we knew. It was a terrible experience." [15]

No master formula can solve the complex motivations of the cult individual. It is true that he was lonely and insecure and that he experienced a growing sense of isolation, frustration, and fear that alienated him toward the society in which he lived. His deep-seated resentment grew increasingly rebellious, yet he knew not where to turn. When he encountered Mankind United, his very smoldering emotions, straining to flare up, made him hypersensitive to its extreme solutions. The concentrated focus of cult activities, the constant repetition, the almost continual meetings and discussions, the lectures upon lectures, the rigidly assigned readings, and the missionary zeal of his fellow workers—all further avalanched his emotional fervor.

But to make uppermost this world of emotions, whether conscious or unconscious, would be to overlook the main impulse motivating the cult individual: viz., his reason. Above all else, he considered himself rational in his actions: his goals must mean something to him. Floating about aimlessly, battered by society, he eagerly seized the lifeline thrown him by Mankind United. It supplied a guide to his understanding. It afforded him the means by which he could act. It offered him a salvation far exceeding mere relief from personal isolation, frustration, and insecurity. It gave him a transcending goal.

Religious Preludes

We go to war—the capitolist [*sic*] goes to church—the soldier takes the gun—the Capitolist takes the profit—while the soldier slays, the Capitolist prays and lays the largest bank bills into the collection plates, and thus public opinion is controlled by the pastor, who willingly blasphemes his own gospel to help promote war for profit.*

Before the cult individual encountered Mankind United, he usually had undergone a long and varied pilgrimage through orthodox churchdom, but nowhere had he found the Holy Grail. His quest left him with slight preference for one denomination over another. All were equally benighted, equally hypocritical, equally impotent. All had accommodated themselves to our evil social, economic, and political system. All were "greedy for gain," with their ministers vainly "sitting in plush seats while the rest of the people sit on hard benches." [16] Even worse, according to the textbook the churches willingly cooperated with the Hidden

---

* *The Old Order Passeth* (Anonymous Mankind United pamphlet, c. 1939), p. 4.

Rulers in duping and exploiting the common people. The cultist caustically labelled their members "lackeys." Prior to his discovery of Mankind United he had picked up a bias against institutionalized religion; within the cult he immediately and wholeheartedly agreed with the common verdict against its "mockery"; after he left the cult, he continued to anathematize "Churchianity" for its perversion of the true meaning of Christianity. In most cases, however, his was not a snap judgment; it was based on diverse, unsatisfying experiences with numerous churches.

A random sample of 117 followers of Mankind United disclosed these earlier denominational affiliations:[17]

Metaphysical (including Christian Science, Unity, New Thought, and Theosophy)	26
Methodist	20
Christian	8
Presbyterian	7
Baptist	7
Roman Catholic	7
Lutheran	5
Mormon (Latter Day Saints)	3
Congregational	3
Kingdom Temple	3
Restored Apostolic Catholic	3
Jehovah's Witnesses	2
Quakers	2
Four-Square Gospel	2
Pentecostal	2
Rosicrucian	2
Swedenborgian	1

Episcopal	1
Evangelical and Reformed	1
Church of Christ	1
Nazarene	1
Chirothesia	1
Clem Davies' Church	1
Lemurian Temple	1
Christ's Sanctified Holiness Church	1
Mentalphysics	1
Campbellite	1
Salvation Army	1
None	3

These categories are according to the follower's principal affiliation. Many, particularly those who called themselves "Metaphysical," had previously passed through two or more denominations.

However, this list only hints at the religious evolution of the cult individual. Looking at his early life, we find that the young cultist-to-be, like the average youth, followed the general religious dictates of his parents; hence he usually attended Sunday school regularly. He was inquisitive and punctilious, often even sensitive. In certain cases he absorbed everything thrust his way by his minister and fervently participated in the church activities: then when the break came, it ordinarily appeared during adolescence. In other cases, unmoved by the dogma, ritual, and teachings of his church, he attended habitually and somewhat lackadaisically, little at variance from the average youth being pressured into the ways of the parental church. But in a majority of cases, the cultist exhibited his rebellious proclivity early, much to the consternation of his mother and father. By and large, it was

his reason, however limited, that defined the emptiness of orthodox Christianity and prompted his decision to break away.

He often claimed, "I did a lot of thinking about religion, even
as a child." Recalling his reactions, he complained that the op-
pressiveness and negativism of his home church had vexed him.
When it had been fundamentalist, his elders, seeing him mature,
had incessantly dwelt on the sinful nature of all men and the
necessity for his conversion, which they expected him to manifest
in front of the congregation. In certain instances he deported
himself as they expected, feigning to be converted, whereupon he
was struck by feelings of guilt and hypocrisy that brought about
an upsurge of strong hostility toward them, ultimately causing
him to leave the church. In other cases when, at adolescence, he
was still unconverted, smarting under the onus, he quietly slipped
out of their midst.

One loyal cult follower, by birth a Southern Methodist, remembered how, as a youth of thirteen, he inhabited the mourn-
ers' bench for two weeks when the revival tent came to his home
town, but despite his efforts, he failed to receive the Holy Ghost.
Looking back at his experience, he opined that those who discuss
the time and place they were "saved" were "liars."

I can't be hypocritical. . . . Once when I was a member of
the church board of a certain Methodist Church, as was the cus-
tom, I served in the choir on Men's Day. The minister named the
seven days of the week, and asked those who had been converted
to stand on the day of the week that they had been blessed by the
Holy Ghost. In the choir I was the only one who was still sitting.
One of those standing said to me, "Why, that's terrible!" Everybody looked at me.[18]

Shortly after, he forsook the church forever. When he subsequently enlisted in Mankind United, he had a chance to fight for

what he felt. "At last I feel I'm doing something," this member concluded.

In another case a former member, born a Presbyterian, disclosed that an evangelist came to her home church when she was twelve and pressed her to be sanctified. "But I couldn't get out of my seat." Thereupon her Sunday school teacher told her that she would go "straight to Hell." Naturally she was terrified. Finding the atmosphere unbearable, she left and attended the Methodist church awhile, but there too something was lacking. "None of them ever greatly appealed to me," she reported. "All the ministers are interested in is the condition of their pocketbooks." She liked to envision a "ladder of life." At the bottom rung of that ladder were the churches. When she left them behind, it was simply because she had climbed beyond them, advancing up another rung in her pursuit of truth. She studied at the Los Angeles Bible Institute; she took to attending lectures; she read voluminously. In the ensuing years she traversed the entire cult domain until finally she thought that she had found her spiritual home in Mankind United, working for six months as a Student Minister, only to be disappointed again.

A third case shows how cultic rebelliousness usually began early and grew more cantankerous with age. Naturally this concerns a dissenter from Mankind United ranks. An elderly widow, she boasted that she was from a well-known, old Virginia family, and she was obviously very proud even though she lived in a rundown shack in a small, out-of-the-way California town. In talking about her childhood she dwelt lengthily on the subject of her two "snooty" sisters, "who always thought they were so nice. . . . I was the black sheep." Reared in a stern religious atmosphere, she claimed that, even as a child, after listening to her local Southern Methodist minister, she would say:

I don't believe that. . . . I don't know why I felt that way. . . . It was just something within me. I can still vividly recall the stories the minister told about damnation and how long many would have to suffer in Hell—burning. . . . Yes, I went through conversion. . . . What a relief it was to wash away the burden of my sins! I didn't leave the Methodist Church, I just seemed to grow out of it, like a snake sheds its skin.[19]

For many years she attended no church. Then she became a rabid student of metaphysics and in the latter part of her sixty-nine years she consumed the writings of practically every cult indigenous to California. Although she severed all association with Mankind United over matters of finance, she remained true to its doctrine, accepting the textbook as her gospel, persisting a cultist to the core.

Biographies of cult followers reveal several common religious experiences that characterized the evolution of the cult individual. Sketched very generally, his history was this: first, he was born into one of the large Protestant denominations. As a matter of family habit he conscientiously attended church, and he often spent his early life in an oppressive religious atmosphere. Always afterward, mordant memories of sin, the Devil, and hell-fire flashed across his mind when he recalled his experience, and he associated these memories, either consciously or unconsciously, with a sense of unknowing fear that he generically called "negativism." Secondly, he confessed to "doing a lot of thinking" about religion during his youth. He resented any church that put restrictions on his intellect or tried to force him into its rigid denominational mold. Simultaneously, willing to act on his beliefs, he often traveled the sawdust trail to the altar to undergo the expected rite of conversion. Thirdly, he manifested an unalloyed alienation toward "Churchianity," accusing it of all manner of perfidy and condemning its pomposity and hypocrisy, and by his late teens he abandoned orthodox Christianity as meaningless and useless. This estrangement was gradual, but decisive and complete. Subsequently his peregrinations carried him to and fro through many esoteric spheres before he alighted on Mankind United. It is clear, therefore, that his response to orthodoxy was the logical extreme—cultism.

As the cult individual grew older, he wanted affirmation and hope from his religion: orthodoxy could give him none. Eventually he contacted Christian Science, Unity, or some other realm of metaphysics, and they released him from his sense of sin, deleted Hell and the Devil from his life, and provided him with a positive, healthy-minded system of thought. Thenceforth he progressed onward and upward, ever searching, far into the stratosphere of the cult and the occult—to pyramidology, astrology, hermetics, spiritualism, faith-healing, Yoga, Lemuria, cabalistic prophecy, or a myriad of others, but not until he happened upon Mankind United did the vision of his cultic dreams come true. There he found satisfactions that no other group had ever given him.

Views and Variations

Countless thousands of Americans have lived through life-situations similar to those experienced by the cult individual without becoming disenchanted with the accepted social, economic, and religious standards around them. The question then arises, "What was the inner impulse that set him off from the mass of ordinary people and moved him to respond actively to cultic views and variations?"

It may be that the cultic mentality lies dormant in a large segment of our population, merely waiting to be stirred by some enterprising cult prophet. Assuredly, "The Voice" of Mankind United hoped for such an awakening. Apparently the fuse that set off the cultist's decision to "do something about it" stemmed from the whole gamut of his previous experiences, religious and otherwise. The moment of his awakening came when he became conscious of himself as an actor in a degenerating world scene, and he did not like his role. A cleavage opened up between his personal standards and the norms of the surrounding society. He wanted a purpose, a goal in life.

The cult follower concluded that life *must* be meaningful. Like the sect followers of history, the substance of his religious search was a need for salvation, but unlike his sect predecessors, he aimed at salvation not only for his group but for all humanity. He was a "World-Saver" who dedicated himself to the cult doctrine that gave his life meaning. His earlier experiences had set forth in stark detail the variation between the ideal and the actual: he chose to act on the ideal. It was in that direction that he foresaw salvation.

It follows that insofar as the Mankind United doctrine was deviant, the thinking of the cult follower was deviant. Nevertheless, he willingly accepted the stigma that the outer world attached to cultic thinking, for he was a missionary, albeit unappreciated, and his zeal was ardent enough to impel him to act on his beliefs. His cultic thought became cultic behavior.

Viewed as a whole, his intellectual make-up was uneven and often contradictory. In some matters, for instance gardening or mechanics, he sometimes was extraordinarily adept, displaying more than average common sense. In juxtaposition, however, when it came to matters cult and occult, he often allied himself with the most aberrant beliefs and attitudes. This antithesis appeared again and again in the cult world.

In view of his deviant tendencies, we might expect the cultist to vary crucially from the outsider. He did. In line with the breach between the cult and the outer world, he habitually colored his thinking either black or white, good or evil, cultic or non-cultic. He demanded extreme answers: the cult gave them to him without hesitation.

In literature, in lectures, and in discussions he found projected before him accounts of the conflict between the powers of Light and Truth and the powers of Darkness and Falsehood. Copious literature proclaimed the dichotomy: "Unjust, power-mad rulers stalk the earth. . . . 'The Babe and the Star' have gone unheeded. . . . The 'lust for power and profit' destroys all that is noble and constructive. . . ." [20] On the side of the Angels were the Sponsors and the followers of Mankind United; on the side of the Devil were the Hidden Rulers and their accomplices. When rebellion broke out in the body of Student Ministers, the dissenting malcontent was officially designated as a "Judas" being used by the legion of evil-doers in their plot to destroy Christ's Church of the Golden Rule. And the utterances of the Prophet ratified this dualistic view of the world.

From what and for what did the cult individual hope to be redeemed? From the world as he experienced and interpreted it; for the New Age incarnate in the Universal Service Corporation. We have seen that, in the course of his intellectual growth, he had been puzzled by many paradoxes in human society: problems of good and evil, wealth and poverty, health and disease, happiness and suffering, war and peace, the young and the elderly— all had impressed themselves on his mind, and a strong desire welled up within him to investigate the causes behind these paradoxes. He felt that orthodox writers on these subjects were intellectually impotent, yet he was convinced that there must be some all-encompassing, underlying answers. Thereupon, when he encountered Mankind United, he was satisfied: he was given absolute explanations for both his personal situation and a diabolical world scene, explanations that provided the logical answers he was looking for.

The Message of Metaphysics

"Matter doesn't matter," quipped a Student Minister who had given up all his material possessions to enter a church project where, among other things, he devoted himself to long hours of study. He was consistent. To his way of thinking, the "selfish mad ambition" that impelled man to serve Mammon and store up material goods was "madness." Behind this belief stood a system of thought called "metaphysics" that was the very heart of Mankind United doctrine. He studied this metaphysics in order to apply it in his day-to-day, project activities. It provided the framework for cultic thinking.

Although the Prophet of Mankind United was admired as a master metaphysician by his disciples, insofar as his revelations consisted of metaphysics, he hardly dispensed a new doctrine. Long before his day, a system of thought, which could scarcely be classified as philosophy or religion in a technical sense, was brewed from many ingredients and given the general name of "metaphysics" by those who formulated it. Among the principal groups espousing this system are the followers of Christian Science, New Thought, Unity, and Theosophy; however, the spark of their metaphysics kindled in the cult world, flaring up more wildly than at its sources, and Mankind United was one of the cults in which it caught fire. It was generally agreed that no single group fully comprehended this system of thought, yet because Christ's Church of the Golden Rule brought its metaphysics into day-to-day application on the projects, it claimed that it had progressed farther than its competitors.

Student Ministers varied greatly in their respective insights into metaphysics and hence in their abilities to apply it. That they be especially intelligent was not mandatory; any sincere person could adhere to it. Inasmuch as few were capable of original contributions to the bulk of metaphysics, the cultists simply accepted and acknowledged it as a framework of thought, no matter how blurred its concepts might seem to them. Student Ministers who strived, whatever their capacities, automatically progressed toward perfection. "The Speaker" bolstered their ego:

> There isn't the tiniest little new worker in our ranks, who isn't a minister of the gospel. If he even lisps this simple truth: "The same size 'guaranteed' pay check for everyone," he is more of a minister than many of the so-called religious leaders we have scattered around the earth today.[21]

To give a synopsis of the essentials of cultic metaphysics presents a major problem because it was exceedingly hazy and elusive. In the first place, there are several things it was not: it was not the negative metaphysics of the Far East that aims at the cessation of all desire; neither did it resemble the technical usage of the philosopher: i.e., "that division of philosophy which includes ontology or the science of being and cosmology, or the science of fundamental causes and processes in things. . . ."[22] Most cultists had never heard of the classical metaphysical systems and, what is more, had little interest in them. To them metaphysics was simply the broad scheme of ideals and principles that gave meaning to the cultic way of life.

Mankind United metaphysics was an amorphous body of knowledge subject to occasional elaborations by Prophet Bell. Engulfing the whole was the concept of "Universal Law," by which was meant the Divine Principle operating in nature and human society. According to this concept, God and the universe are fundamentally spiritual, and God works through Universal Laws, utilizing them in shaping the brute mass of nature and continually unfolding their truths to man. In this monistic system, God becomes impersonal; God becomes pantheistic, filling all space; in effect, God becomes Universal Law, the Prime Mover, the Omniscient, Omnipotent, Omnipresent Creator, who established and maintains the laws of the universe. Nominally Christian, yet syncretic in its outlook, metaphysics appealed to those repelled by the Christian concepts of Heaven and Hell, and at the same time it retained the general Christian ethic of the New Testament, insofar as Jesus was a master teacher of Universal Laws. Indeed, Jesus was the foremost exemplar of the Universal Ideals of Love, Wisdom, and Brotherhood. He was the great "Way Show-er."

According to this metaphysical thought, the physical world is merely a form of mind: God is mind; Man is mind. Similarly, God is Good; Evil is the absence of Good (God). It follows that Sin amounts simply to man's mistakes; Hell is wherever God (Good) and Truth are absent. Hence, Error manifests itself only when a person allows himself to believe it can exist. To emancipate himself, he need only awaken from his "Adam dream of materiality" and acknowledge that God is everything. There can be no error beyond what a person allows himself to believe, and consequently he has it within his power to exterminate that which is unlike God, including the material, from his situation. To alter his external situation, he need only to alter his thinking.

All limitation derives from human error. Discordant belief has no place in the Divine Mind, existing only in the human mind. When error is driven out of the human consciousness, the only place where it exists, then it evaporates into nothingness. Evidently the cultists were positive that there was no limit to what they could do if they utilized metaphysical law properly. Notes taken at meetings reveal that

Man is to become a superman . . . stretch yourself beyond human capacity. Have the Divine Will back of it.[23]

Ten people can perform this miracle if their consciousness is expanded. . . . Those with a true sense of "no lack" are the ones to build the New Order. The world says we can't do this but we are not interested in what the world says. We are using Universal Law to get this program.[24]

Metaphysical concepts were closely interlaced with astrology, spiritualism, occultism, reincarnation, secret rays, even death, and the main avenue for cross-fertilization was the theory of "vibrations" generally held by the cultists. "Good" (Love) was a "high vibration rate"; "Evil" (Hate) was a "low vibration rate." Somewhat hazily they entertained ideas about a central sun exuding varying rates of vibrations that were the essence of life. Let a Mankind United lecturer clarify the matter:

There is the Universal substance from which all things are made, and in the last analysis thoughts are vibrations; and if we hold in consciousness an atom vibrating in the substance of our desire, by intensifying that desire we attract by the same atoms all the same vibrations, then lowering our mental vibration until a thought pattern becomes visible in the form of matter.[25]

Therefore man should strive to become conscious of the good, high vibration rates, thus becoming "God-conscious." Every person gives off an "aura" of vibrations, a sort of spectrum, that may extend in range from the ultra-low rates of black magic to the ultra-high rates of God-consciousness. Needless to say, in the case of the Hidden Rulers the vibration rate of their auras was extremely low. One cult member, a vegetarian, further refined this aura-theory by proclaiming: "No one can become spiritual who eats flesh: when he eats his fill of meat he takes on the lower animal vibrations. . . . No one can be on a spiritual plane and an animal plane at the same time." [26]

"The stars weren't put up there just to look at. They control our lives," cultists often announced. The astrological concept of ascending planes was common parlance in California cult circles, and combined with metaphysics, it explained such cultic phenomena as the translevitating powers of Prophet Bell. A "Doctor of Mentalphysics" claimed this insight:

We have three bodies: the physical, the astral, and the cosmic. The astral body is the one by which Mr. Bell might leave his body. It's quite possible. I've done it myself. You can go anywhere in the world. . . . I have a sixth sense by which I can see the astral body of a patient separate from the physical. I refuse those patients. I know they are soon to die, and I would be blamed. I can intuitively judge the condition of vibrations . . . I can see right into you. . . . [27]

Intertwined with the concept of ascending planes was the idea of reincarnation, which received almost unqualified endorsement from the cultist. Here he deviated most widely from orthodox Christian dogma. Frequently he attested to a strange consciousness:

Things have come into my mind from previous incarnations. I dream of being a hairy thing—squat . . . I remember wearing a coat of mail on a previous Atlantis.[28]

There have been three times that something has happened to me that had happened before in a different body. One time I was paralyzed for ten minutes. Those who have experienced this know what I mean.[29]

Reincarnation was also closely related to the metaphysical theory of vibrations. It was held that the vibrations permeating the universe were indestructible and what is more, cumulative. Each soul automatically advanced. In death it merely trans-levitated itself, either to another body or to another plane. In his parting message to his cult followers, Prophet Bell revealed that for years secret equipment in the subterranean laboratories of the International Institute of Universal Research and Administration had been detecting the vibration rates of loyal Uniters of Mankind, and that this self same equipment, by slightly altering their vibration rate and atomic structure, would, at the moment of their death, bring about their transition to another planet.

This theory of vibrations also applied to matters of personal health, where the cult individual embraced the mind-cure doctrine, i.e., the idea that by entertaining good thoughts of high vibration rate he could eliminate all physical ailments. Pain, suffering, and disease exist only in the thoughts of man. Consequently, the cultist had only to correct the error of his thinking and harmonize with Universal Law, which permits no ill health or suffering, and automatically all his physical and mental illnesses would fade away.

These Universal Laws apply to every conceivable phase of

human and natural existence. No situation is outside their jurisdiction. Nobody has ever formulated all of them, and entire
books have been written on each of them. Every metaphysician
had his favorite set. Following are a few of the principal ones
in Mankind United.

First of all, there was the unerring "Law of Cause and
Effect," which adjusts each effect to its cause on all planes
of human experience—physical, mental, and spiritual. Thus
thoughts of hate return suffering to their producer; thoughts of
love, nothing but blessings. Fully as important was the "Universal Law of Love." Derived from the command to "Love thy
neighbor as thyself," this Law could now be practicably applied
to all human affairs if the ways and means of the Mankind
United program were adopted. Then there was the "Universal
Law of Adjustment," which was inherent in the Golden Rule and
practiced on the church projects. And finally, the "Universal
Law of Abundance" defined the true meaning of money and
showed that the right attitude of thought was crucial for the
success of the Mankind United program. In line with the cultic
preoccupation with the ideal rather than the actual, each law
stressed the purely mental, rather than the physical, aspects of
reality.

"Thoughts are things," they were told. "If there seems to
be confusion and disorder among us . . . it must be because
of our own lack of orderly thinking." [30] The Uniters of Mankind,
under the "Leadership of Eternal Right Ideas," sought to apply
certain central concepts to all areas of social, political, and economic life. Supposedly their cultic creed derived from four main
sources: the Golden Rule; the Sermon on the Mount; the Ten
Commandments; the Constitution of the United States. Only by
practicing Universal Law could they apply this creed to the

world scene. This was the essence of the Mankind United crusade. It is significant that their leader was known as "The Voice of the Right Idea," who once told them that "THE FATE OF OUR CIVILIZATION LIES IN THE HANDS OF TODAY'S THINKERS!" [31]

Yet there were deep-seated inconsistencies in their thinking that disturbed the mental assuredness of the cult individual. Of these the most baffling was the age-old problem of Evil. Metaphysics tolerated no Evil: Evil was no actual thing—only an illusion fabricated by a blurred mentality. How then could the Mankind Uniter explain the Hidden Rulers, those real, flesh and blood evil-doers, and the brutal, factual suffering in the present world situation? In a quandary, he sometimes squirmed out with "The Hidden Rulers simply ignore their Creator. Consequently, they are not the Evil, the Evil is their ignorance, which is not a reality." [32]

Despite the demands of metaphysics, he retreated into the aforementioned dualistic view of the world, colored black and white, a nether world of conflict and paradox. He rationalized that since good thoughts can create health, similarly, evil thoughts can produce illness, even in others. Ultimately this concept gave birth to a form of modern witchcraft—viz., a widespread cultic belief in black magic. He explained that "When the mind is used for evil, it is what you call 'black magic.'" [33] Whenever a present or past cult member ran into any sort of trouble or was taken seriously ill, gossip flew about black magic, its ominous threat hanging heavily over the tense cult atmosphere.

Although not all that was metaphysical was beautiful, to many Student Ministers the metaphysics still constituted the greenest intellectual pasture in the cult field. When they renounced their allegiance to the outer world and entered a church project, they often did so with the idea of devoting themselves to studying the "Spiritual." In the latter years some of the most fervid affiliates were those dedicated to illustrating the Universal Laws in their project life. Concomitantly, others equally attracted to metaphysics decided, as a result of their experiences, that Christ's Church of the Golden Rule failed to operate according to Universal Law, and, disillusioned, they returned to the outside world.

SHADOWS OF HEAVEN

People must have hope. They must have a purpose in life, otherwise they might as well be dead or commit suicide. . . . Our mission was to bring Heaven: to show the world that Christ's teachings would work economically.

There was an adventurous spirit about the crusade.

Everybody was thrilled.

Everybody thought they were an ambassador bringing a New Age.*

This California cultist little resembled his compatriots among the sects of the disinherited, such as Jehovah's Witnesses, who follow the millennial scheme of the Book of Revelation. Seldom did he employ the Biblical language of the Apocalypse. Neither did his hope for paradise rest in the coming of the Son of Man to exterminate the wicked and relieve a suffering humanity. Although it was true that Biblical prophecy would be fulfilled, he announced, "I don't believe that God is going to come with his chariot to do it as some fanatics do." [34] Instead, he placed his

---

* Excerpts from personal interviews with different Student Ministers in Christ's Church of the Golden Rule.

faith in a present-day, corporate messiah, Mankind United. Before its exodus from the California cult scene, he awaited the glorious day when its Sponsors would usher in the 30-day Program as eagerly as the early Christian anticipated the imminent return of Jesus Christ to usher in the Messianic Age.

Much of the attraction of Mankind United lay in the fact that not the past, but the present was the history-making era, and not Palestine, but California was the holy land. "You live in one of the great revolutionary moments in history," [35] the cult leader told him. The Manager of the "Ray of Light" Bureau added:

Each one of you have the honor of living in an age when humanity is promised a great Cosmic uplift. Great Changes will usher in the fulfilment of the Divine Plan. The prophesy of the Bible, the Great Pyramid, Clairvoyant interpretation, the Heavenly bodies, the Masters of old,—not to mention the evidence of our senses at the trend of each day's events—all declare that the fulfilment of the Christian Cycle is about to take place— and all things shall be made new. Unless all these things are wrong and we are a group of senseless fanatics, we are to behold the days of miracles. . . .[36]

The cult individual felt no doubt about the imminence of the Day of Judgment. For years cult literature and cult Prophet unremittingly hammered home the prognostication that the cosmic die was cast and that everything pointed to the advent of a New Age. The Sponsors confirmed these views, and even more convincing was the evidence of metaphysics. Since Universal Law controls all events, Universal Law unfolding is the process of history. Consequently, in contrast with the Christian doctrine of historical decay, his faith lay in historical progress. His *Weekly Message* told him:

The Law of Progress has never at any time been slowed down nor curbed by any of the antics of the human mind. . . . There is nothing that can prevent Mankind's awakening from the Adam Dream of Materiality. We are in the front-line trenches with those who are breaking the age-old superstitions of limitation. . . .[37]

During the declining days of the cult, however, especially during the disintegration of Christ's Church of the Golden Rule, an admixture of many colors showed up in cultic thinking. Still clinging to the Law of Progress, but cognizant of deteriorating world conditions, the cultist painted the future blacker and blacker. "The old age is gone. This is a time of 'very much crisis,'"[38] he stated. He saw the world heading toward a final cataclysm engulfing all aspects of life, political, economic, and even geographical. He stoically asserted that the human race must suffer. In the words of one cultist:

The only way to bring about a permanent change in our civilization is for about three-fourths of our people to be killed in a terrible war. The Jewish International Bankers that control the world's money will join the Russian Communists to rule the world, fifty-fifty. They will fight against the United States and other powers. I look for all our cities to be wiped out within the space of four hours by bombers coming over the North Pole. The A-bomb and gas will be used. It will be necessary to flee to the mountains. That is going to happen. . . .[39]

Accompanying this Armageddon was to occur a stupendous geographical upheaval, according to the thinking of some cultists. One proclaimed that he knew of at least twenty persons besides himself who had dreamt that Southern California was going to sink into the Pacific Ocean.[40] Another subscribed to the same feelings: "'They that know about that' say the poles are about to shift. . . . There is a major fault passing through California. All that is west of there is going to sink. You can't tell where you'll be safe." [41] This was another reason for abandoning the planet Earth.

The tiny, loyal remnant of Mankind Uniters, as we have seen, still had hope. Abiding on their church projects, practicing their metaphysics, they complacently awaited their metamorphosis, through secret cult devices, to the Universal Service Corporation—on another world.

But what about those thousands of ex-members of Mankind United who, having lost their faith in its mission, now had no hope for a future resurrection? Disillusioned, they often avowed that never again would they have anything to do with a similar group, but in spite of that fact, they continued to pursue their reading and research in the realm of metaphysics and the occult. Almost never did they rebound into orthodox Christianity. Instead, for example, one of them might disclose confidentially that a friend of his belonged to the Lemurian Brotherhood, and having heard that the Lemurians were behind the flying saucers, he thought he might look into their ideas. In fact, he might already have pledged his allegiance to them.

Of a naturally inquisitive intellect, the dissenting cult individual was not made for a celibate life—he thrived best when wedded to the kind of logic found only in cult circles. Although he often castigated Prophet Bell and Christ's Church of the Golden Rule, surprisingly, he was not an ideological dissenter. He still affirmed that the basic Mankind United plan was perfect; he continued to assent to the ideals and principles in the cult doctrine and was convinced that its solution was the only solution for the ills of the world. Even though dissenting, he held to this opinion.

His favorable opinion also extended to his former comrades in the cult venture. Almost always he praised them exorbitantly: "They were the best people I ever met. . . . You never met a finer, more idealistic group of people anywhere. . . . The highest grade of people. . . . Our bureau contained the most idealistic, the most dedicated, the finest people I have ever known." [42] What is more significant, even after he severed all connections with Mankind United, he still maintained friendships that flowered in the intimate gardens of the cult. These people were his kind of people: he was lonely for thinkers that agreed with him, and he had many common memories to talk over with them.

Convinced that doomsday was almost here, however, he grimly bided his time, hoping against hope that in these last years of world history there might appear in the heavens a cultic star heralding the birth of a new prophet with a last-minute reprieve for civilization. Meanwhile he bowed to fate and accepted a pessimistic pattern of things to come. To his way of thinking, humanity had not advanced far enough to avert the catastrophe that was about to explode in its face.

Just as the image of an ideal Heaven gave meaning to the world of medieval man, so the image of the Universal Service Corporation had given meaning to the world of this twentieth-century man. When his vision of utopia dimmed, the venture into utopia waned. His world slowly turned to ashes. He awaited the fall of man.

Appendix A: *Notes on Theory*

The author has assumed the commonly held premise that the social sciences join forces with psychology at the level of the concrete case. It is when we can answer the question, "How does the cultist feel, what does he think, and what are his goals?" that we can begin to understand cult phenomena. Hence, much of the key probing was done at the personal level.

For turning his back on organized society the cult member stands convicted of deviant behavior. He failed to fit into the mold shaped by our institutions. Why? We have taken the position that, while psychological mechanisms can be used to account for his aberrancy, a gap exists between them and a well-rounded interpretation of cult behavior. Into the latter enters the subjective element of meaning, intention, and purpose which falls outside the boundaries of analytical psychology. Max Weber maintained that the "actual subjective intention" (*subjectiv gemeinter Sinn*) of the acting individual is the basic postulate by which we can gain understanding of social behavior. Pertinent to this concept were the reactions of the cult member at various levels of motivation.

At the top level we have attempted to analyze his cognitive activity, that in which he reasoned out his personal situation and related it to his view of the world. Next came consideration of his emotional life, his world of sentiments and their effect on his behavior. Finally we have turned to his unreflective reactions, often unconsciously revealed, that resulted from the commands of habit, tradition, and early conditioning. Note that in each of these levels there is a weakening influence of the rational element.

It is critical to an understanding of cult behavior, as *verstehen* implies, that we ascertain the effect that the individual rationally expected to result from his behavior. Consequently, instead of an emphasis upon intrinsic psychological motivations, the author has tended to stress the manifest intellectual life of the cultist.

Above all else, the cult member considered himself rational in his actions; his goals had to mean something to him. Before entering Mankind United, he had suffered under the tension that accompanied this unresolved desire for meaning. He was annoyed, bothered, dangling. In Durkheimian parlance, he was the victim of that disintegrated frame of mind called *anomie*. The cult supplied him with a guide to understanding and afforded him the means by which he could act upon his situation. Since he felt alienated toward the accepted ethos of his culture, when the cult ship of Mankind United came into view and provided him with a direction and goal that seemed reasonable to him, he eagerly climbed aboard and bent his back to the oars.

In analyzing Mankind United as an ideal type of modern cult, the author has combined three divergent frames of reference: first, we have looked at the cult organism and the individual member from the point of view of the objective observer. In the panorama of American life Mankind United had little historical importance. Yet, the growth of modern cults is significant to the disciplines of the social sciences. The first value of Mankind United lay in the fact that it afforded an ideal construct of this type of modern cult—its structure, its doctrine, its leadership, and its community life. Fitting into the tradition of American aberrant thought, the group is not an isolated phenomenon but an integral part of the rationalistic secularization of American society. Secondly, we have investigated the technique by which the cult conditioned its members—its method of operation. How did the cult hierarchy, from the cult leader down, govern the group? How did it maintain its authority over the membership? How did its bureaucracy operate? How did it react to surrounding society? Thirdly, we have delineated the cult individual, i.e., the ideal type of all-out adherent to Mankind United, describing his personality, personal history, views, goals, subjective reactions, and mental make-up. When abstracting the characteristics of the cult individual, the author has not attempted to describe the average type of member; no person with all the stipulated characteristics actually existed. This ideal type involves a one-sided exaggeration of reality useful as an extreme picture from which comparisons and contrasts can be drawn.

At the same time that the cult organism is approached as an ideal type, its elements—i.e., the cult prophet, the cult individual, the literature, the discipline, the myth, the cult community, cult finance, cult doctrine, and relations with the world —are examined both as integral parts of Mankind United and as abstracted subtypes characteristic of modern cultism.

Appendix B: *Research Materials*

When the author arrived on the southern California scene in the fall of 1946 looking for an extremist cult that would serve as an intimate case study, he happened upon a rich cache of research materials at the State House in Los Angeles. Because of complaints received from ex-members of Mankind United who desired to retrieve the property that they had deeded to it, the California Attorney General, alleging fraudulent operations, had forced the cult into State bankruptcy courts. While collecting information and materials with which to prepare the State's case, a staff of special investigators and assistant attorney generals had unwittingly performed much spadework that could be utilized for an academic study of Mankind United. These materials were made available to the author.

Working from this foundation, the author devoted nearly two years, from late 1946 to early 1948, to firsthand field work that took him throughout the State. There were numerous sources of information: the files of the Attorney General's office, transcripts of public hearings, transcripts of court proceedings, attendance of bankruptcy court hearings, transcripts of State legislative committee reports before which different members of the cult had testified, copies of notes on lectures and meetings taken years before by ex-members, newspaper-clipping files, religious questionnaires submitted to the upper hierarchy of the cult, and an assortment of self records (such as biographical essays, individual digests of cult literature, and personal sermons by cult adherents). Most important of all, the author personally observed the cult situation through visits to various operating church projects, and on numerous occasions he conducted personal interviews with the cult leader, the "loyal affiliates" of the group, and the "dissenters" who had withdrawn into the outside world.*

None of this source material is on deposit in any established library, and consequently, except as former members might have saved it, or as the Attorney General's office may have preserved vital sections of it, references made to it in footnotes are to be found only in the files of the author. Most of the cult literature lists a publication date. Because of the emphasis upon impersonalism, many of the tracts are anonymous, but others indicate their authorship in titles containing one of the noms de plume of the cult leader.

The textbook of the cult, titled *Mankind United*, failed to list an author, giving the copyright date of 1934 by "The International Registration Bureau." According to a California legislative committee transcript** the book was copyrighted by "L. Osborne," one of the aliases used by Arthur L. Bell. Nevertheless, the cult leader disclaimed authorship, stating that he merely edited the book and that the information in it was assembled by "many people." In 1937 a second book, *The Time is Short, A Plan for Economic Salvation*, was published by "The International Registration Bureau," also of anonymous authorship. A smaller book, it was intended to supplement *Mankind United* and never became as popular in cult circles as the original textbook.

Throughout the cult history, especially the later phases, the most widely circulated literature took the form of mimeographed tracts. Some were administrative directives, often bearing standard titles such as *Dept. "A" Bulletin; Division Superintendent's*

---

* See Appendix C.
** Assembly Fact-Finding Committee on Un-American Activities in California, Jack B. Tenney, Chairman. March 20, 1944.

Remarks; Speaker's Remarks; Church Trustee's Letter; Project Instruction Bulletins, etc. These were sent out whenever the occasion demanded and were dated accordingly. A bibliography of these bulletins published by the cult listed 119 titles circulating between January 1943 and May 1946. Other pamphlets were published regularly, either weekly or monthly. Foremost among these were the *Weekly Messages,* which began their mimeographed existence on October 20, 1941. Others were called *Tools; Letters from a World Saver to his Son; Magic Touch; Electric Shock; Nu'Era Beacon; Cream Drops; Reflections; Rainbow Hues of New Age Views; Unfoldment;* and *Junior Weekly Messages.*

All of these tracts were widely circulated, filed in personal notebooks, and pondered over on many subsequent occasions by the cult members. As sources of information concerning the myth and doctrine of the cult, they were second only to the textbook itself.

Appendix C: *Notes on Interview Technique*

Before taking to the field, the author drew up several interview guides: first, an objective schedule involving basic personality patterns and personal history; and second, a more specific guide involving reactions at higher levels of motivation, dealing with attitudes, beliefs, views, and goals.* These guides were made up after the author had perused the California Attorney General's files, taking notes on the relevant data. From this material he constructed a reasonably clear picture of the structure of Mankind United and the mentality of its adherents, and he was able partly to project himself into the cult situation and experience the emotional context that it involved. At the same time he visited the Mankind United bankruptcy hearings then being held in a Los Angeles Federal courtroom, here too imbibing some of the emotions as well as some of the definitions of the cultists. These experiences provided the interviewer with a pre-analysis somewhat broader than the perspective of the cult individual.

One of the most time-consuming of all tasks was that of gaining an entree into the good graces of the cult leader. Always hustling, he was accessible only for a few minutes on certain days after the court proceedings had ended. When the author introduced himself, Mr. Bell exclaimed, "From Harvard? Isn't that the place where all the Communists come from?" He always qualified his attitude toward the author according to his sus-

* Cf. Appendix A, *Notes on Theory*.

139

picions that here might be an undercover F.B.I. agent with
bogus credentials from Harvard University.

In spite of his suspicions, some sort of rapport with the cult
leader was necessary. Only with his explicit permission was the
author permitted to visit certain of the church projects in operation and talk with a closely screened portion of the loyal
members. None of them would talk to any outsider unless Mr.
Bell gave specific sanction, and then only in the presence of a
second loyal member. They had been repeatedly told, and the
cult literature reiterated: "There is no slightest excuse for anyone associated with our church ever discussing anything pertaining to this work, its teachings, its business activities, its finances,
or anything else directly or indirectly associated with our activities with outsiders. . . ." What they said was usually quite
guarded, and the product of reflection as to possible subsequent effects. In making an interviewing call on them, the author
completed all arrangements beforehand, permitting them to
choose the setting. Naturally this interviewing situation was far
from ideal, but it was the best possible that a strange investigator,
automatically suspect in their eyes, could expect from them.

Most of the dissenting members, having left the cult community, were willing to talk about their feelings and experiences.
Approaching them was simple. The author simply appeared without warning and rang doorbells, thus eliminating the possibility
of being refused a telephone appointment. Happily, circumstance
granted that most of the interviewing relationships soon reached
a friendly level. Only two refused to talk. Names and addresses
of dissenting members came from various sources: the Attorney
General's office, transcripts of court hearings, publication by Mankind United authorities of a list of "Judases" with whom no loyal

member was to have any speech or contact of any kind under penalty of excommunication, and finally, leads from ex-members, once the interviewing had begun.

When talking with the interviewee, the author was able to compare his pre-analysis with the statements made by the cultist and note the discrepancies. And there were discrepancies. Since the cultist abhorred all "wrong thinking," he would go to any length to save his intellectual face. The author did not feel it incumbent to judge him, however; neither was the interview intended to cure a psychoneurotic patient by means of a kind of confessional or free association or counseling. Hence, no effort was made to point out inconsistencies.

At the beginning the interviewee might be willing to talk only of a certain phase of his cult beliefs. At this point the author, making no effort to bring up any particular topic, tried merely to instil confidence in the subject to talk. As the interview continued, however, the cultist went deeper into his intellectual secrets and personal background, often feeling impelled to carry his revelations into remoter fields. In time, he elicited deeply emotional and value-laden remarks, some of central and some of peripheral significance. In this exploration backwards, the interviewer strived to bring up questions related to the feeling-tones manifested by the person on specific cult matters. Often the interviewee pried into areas that he had never before articulated.

In so far as it was feasible, the author encouraged a mood of retrospective introspection, i.e., by verbally re-creating some noteworthy event in the history of the cult, he tried to encourage the interviewee to recapture his thoughts and reactions concerning the event at the time it occurred. In addition, the interviewer occasionally cast out suggestions concerning the way the cultist may have felt previously, and in having his feeling content answered, the cultist usually felt that he was being deeply understood and tended to unveil his sentiments more fully.

All told, excluding his many talks with the cult leader, the author conducted ninety-five interviews among seventy-four different persons, twenty-six loyal members and forty-eight dissenting members. The settings were impromptu in the case of the dissenters, and, as previously mentioned, predetermined in the case of the loyalists. Interviews varied in length, generally lasting between two and three hours, with the termination mutually governed. Immediately afterwards, they were written up with wording and phrasing as close as possible to the interviewee's own. Sometimes, when an individual case was sufficiently pertinent and interesting, two or three interviews were held. From the first, the author made it plain to the interviewees that no personal embarrassment could possibly come from the conversations. Consequently, whenever the occasion has demanded in order to protect the individual involved, he has disguised names and settings—without interfering, however, with the general truth and scientific validity of the narrative.

These personal case studies were the primary basis for constructing an image of the cult individual.

Appendix D: *Two Typical Cultists*

To reconstruct past personal behavior is always difficult: there are many obstacles, not the least of which are memory lapses, emotional colorings, and subsequent rationalizations. However, to get at certain factors motivating the cult individual, let us attempt to cut through these obstacles and look at several detailed case histories in which early conditioning undoubtedly underlay adult participation in cult activities. These are the cases of "Leonard" and "Louise."

Leonard *

Leonard was an extreme cult type. Forty-four years old, he suffered ill-health much of his life, and he ruefully brought forth recollections of many mishaps and illnesses. When he was only two years old, he was dropped and suffered a broken arm. A "drunken doctor" set it incorrectly, and it grew somewhat deformed. Later at different intervals he came down with a severe attack of pneumonia, required several serious operations, and twice was struck down by rheumatic fever. His sixteen years of marital life with a "wayward" wife terminated in divorce. In addition to these afflictions, he told of several serious accidents out of which he had emerged unscathed, each time adding the

* Constructed from a series of personal interviews totaling approximately fourteen hours.

143

postscript, "I feel God was with me. I figure there must have been some reason I came out unhurt."

The son of strict German-Lutheran immigrants, Leonard received an ultraconservative early religious training that appears to have shaped his whole ensuing life. Generously scattered throughout his speech were hazy Biblical quotations. Significant also were the several traumata, with ministers playing leading roles, which he related with incandescent feelings. It is interesting psychologically that religion and sex combined in his most vivid childhood memories.

When he was six, staying in his home town with an aunt while going to school, he was impressed by "what dirty people the ministers and their children were." He was shocked to discover that his own pastor chewed tobacco. Leonard condemned the use of tobacco and alcoholic beverages all his life. What is more, while staying with this aunt, he heard that one of the other ministers of the town (not his own pastor) had "put one of the prettiest girls I've ever seen, only fourteen, in a family way. That's the kind of people they are."

Later he was confirmed and attended church loyally. "It meant a lot to me," he recalled. But then he began to hear lurid moral tales about his own minister, tales concerning nudity and rape of the organist, a banker's daughter. About this time, too, the same pastor placed a confession box in the rear of the church and asked his flock to write out their sins and deposit them in it. Infuriated by this "last straw," Leonard vowed that he would never go back to that church. When his family remonstrated with him, he countered, "Why should I confess my sins to a sinful man like that?"

He never entered an orthodox church after that. Lumping all denominations together, he commented:

They're all part of the money system; any rich person in the congregation can control what the minister says. Preachers don't have the backbone to stand up and say what they actually think. I got a Methodist minister to read *Mankind United*, and after he had gone through it he said it was the most revealing book next to the Bible that he'd ever read. Then I asked him to read parts of it from his pulpit on Sunday mornings and he was aghast. "I couldn't do that," he said, "I'd lose my job." That's what's wrong with our clergy. They're working at a job. They get a little more education than the rest of us, become smooth talkers, and then take it easy in their good job. They don't have to get out and sweat like the rest of us.

"Both my parents always treated me fine," he added. His mother, intent upon instilling him with Christian ideals, was most strict about his attending Sunday school and always wielded a powerful influence over him. Then, when he was fourteen, she was killed in an automobile accident. Leonard picked up her dead body. "It still stands in my memory as though it was yesterday," he reminisced. "Looking over the scene of the accident, I'm sure that God ordained that my mother die then, for otherwise how would a heavy Oldsmobile turn over lengthwise from hitting a six-inch rut in the road?"

Another item stood out in his memory. At the age of seven he was taken to hear William Jennings Bryan at a nearby Chatauqua meeting. There Bryan orated that "Most people have the minds of a fifteen-year-old." This statement clung to his mind throughout the years following when, in the course of his varied experiences, he had many proofs of the brutality and animality of human beings. "People are so foolish and selfish," he once remarked. "They stand like cows, fearing the world situation, but will they do anything about it?"

The setting of Leonard's formative years was pious, first

generation, rural South Dakota. It was a simple and severe life. Apparently its inflexible moralistic coloring gave a bleak, gray tint to all of his subsequent thinking. He was looking for something, and, as he grew older, his intellectual interests broadened to encompass the realm of economics, metaphysics, and things cultic. But his search ended in fatalism, for he finally admitted, "I am sure that a person's life is pretty well mapped out for him when he is born. I feel that all of my experiences have added up to building the point of view I now have."

Although he wanted an education, Leonard had to quit school in the fifth grade to help his father work the family farm in central South Dakota. In his late teens he left home and became a "drifter," passing through a typical variety of ordinary jobs. He worked on railroad section gangs, fired locomotives, spent a peacetime term in the army, rode the rails having to beg for handouts, did odd jobs on a dude ranch, drove a cleaning truck, worked for an oil company, tried truck farming, and even spent a couple of years bootlegging during Prohibition days.

Firing the engines on the railroad was the toughest job. On some runs I'd shovel twenty tons of coal. I've seen the way railroad workers act and think. I drank with them. I had fights with them. I whored with them. They're ruled only by force. They have no morals. They take on the first woman they come to. That's another reason I think God must have been with me. On one occasion after getting off the train in Sioux City nine of us men took on one woman. Six of these got gonorrhea; I was one of the three that didn't. I figure there must have been some reason for that. Those men have no understanding of what is happening to them or to the world today. They are satisfied only to get enough to eat and enough sex. It was there I first learned how base humans really are.

Not only have I been "on the bum" all through the United States, I've also gone up into Canada and down into Mexico. I saw the way the lower fourth of the people live. There's no reason for them to live the way they do. I didn't realize it then. I do now. Everything could be changed by four o'clock this afternoon if those people would only act, but no, they go on their dull way. We would have to change our money system. Have you ever read the book, *Medical Mussolinis?* That's a fine book. It tells how the medical profession dopes the populace while horrible conditions prevail. They're part and parcel of the whole system. Why is it that when people have that kind of truth set forth before their eyes, they continue on as they do? That is the reason I have become disgusted with human nature. They don't seem to want to learn.

I volunteered for the army in the twenties, and that also taught me that man is essentially a beast. I saw how men are regimented, and I knew that it was part of the profit system. I always had brushes with the brass. I wouldn't accept stripes . . . always managed to get them taken away if I did.

I went "bad" when I got out . . . led a wild life . . . ran whiskey for "Sadie" in Sioux City . . . made $2,000 a month for almost a year. I feel God must have meant this experience to be a part of my lessons in life. It was while bootlegging that I first came to realize that the material is unimportant: it gives no lasting pleasure. I made a lot of money but I spent it all. Most people today are like I was then—dumb brutes. They don't think what they're doing nor why. They just exist. It is disillusioning that when you talk to them and try to give them the truth, they call you a "crackpot."

I've tried truck farming in Oregon . . . got several acres of Beaver Dam land, the richest in the country . . . tried to raise onions but smut and cutworm ruined my crops. It's just like gambling. Prices in 1930 were $11.00 a hundred, next year they were 90¢ per hundred. What is the reason or justice in that? I've seen large Bartlett pears a foot deep on the ground under trees, rotting, not worth enough to pick them up. The large canneries wouldn't buy them, and they kept the little fellow from trying to can and sell them by having him prosecuted under their strict Pure Food Act. What chance does the little fellow have against a man with a million dollars? A key slogan in my life has come to be: "Those who have shall be given to; those who have not shall be taken from."

Throughout it all he nursed the singular ambition to become a stationary engineer, but he explained, "In school I always had trouble with fractions. . . . Still, I can do engineering work that the so-called 'licensed' engineers cannot do, but they have memorized their little answers out of books and can pass the test. So they get the license. I can't. There isn't any justice in that either."

After his uninterrupted series of frustrations, he entered the Mankind United sphere. What first attracted him was the textbook itself. "I never have come across anything before or since that so completely explains the reason for all the hardship and discord I have seen in the world." Even after leaving the Church he declared that he agreed with it one hundred percent, holding it next only to the Bible in truth.

Yes, I believe in the Sponsors. They operate in hidden ways that none of us know. There must have been a smart group of men behind such a movement as Mankind United; one man couldn't have started it himself. With my own eyes I've seen some of the inventions they have . . . a very compact electrical machine that could light a whole city. Have you heard about the machine that a farmer up in San Jose invented? By plugging it into an ordinary light socket, this gadget, the size of a small table radio, could destroy all vegetation on a mountain twenty miles away. The army wouldn't even bother to come out to see it. Henry Ford sent one of his men out, who reported that it was perfect, but it would put munition makers out of business. Anyway, the invention was shelved. Big business always does that. There are so many wonderful inventions that are bought up and stored away by big companies. Why should our government keep those inventions locked up in the Patent Office? Why shouldn't they be used to lighten the burden of the working man? He wouldn't have to work more than four hours a day, four days a week. It's just because a few people, the Hidden Rulers, are selfish.

Arthur L. Bell? He's a very brilliant and clever man. I've learned a lot of metaphysics from him. I could sit for hours and listen to him. Sure he had doubles and could transport himself anywhere. All that's required is power of mind. When you were excited or nervous and he looked at you, he could make you become calm and collected. That was his influence, just through his eyes. He was wonderful!

Subsequently he gave everything he possessed to Christ's Church and for eighteen months worked on a hotel project.

I was willing to give my all, for it appeared that here was to be an example of the concrete application of Christ's teachings. I still support those ideals. But the people on the projects did not live up to them. Some of the project managers treated the people like slaves. One of them treated me as though I was dirt and I offered to fight him and have it out. That set me to thinking. They were too narrow-minded. They squabbled, back-bited, and quarreled.

After his disillusionment he left the Church, "no longer caring for anything of that kind," and he took no further interest in any cult group.

Needing an idealistic goal to lift him out of his doldrums and give his life a purpose, Leonard thought that at last he had found a spiritual home in Mankind United, and he went all-out for its program. But even it proved wanting. "It gradually came to me," he continued, "that the people in it betrayed the ideals and principles. I realized they were not yet ready for it. . . ." Apathetic and broken in spirit, he no longer felt he was "getting anywhere," even in the cult world, and ultimately he simply did

not care. His is a case where the relation between means and
ends were wholly upset. He suffered from an advanced stage
of *anomie*.

Once on the outside, he took the first job that came his way,
that of a combination assistant cook and dishwasher in a small
café. "I didn't care to do anything but just to get along," he
then said. "I've had a chance to get any number of good jobs,
but I'm getting in a rut; I don't seem to want to do anything but
exist." At last report, to flee the impending atomic catastrophe
that "everything points to," he planned to get a job as a hand
on a Nevada dude ranch. Why? "It will be a good place to be
in the times ahead. . . . The Battle of Armaggedon hasn't been
fought yet. It will be."

*Louise**

Louise was another case where early personal experiences
undoubtedly aided in bringing about her later interest in cult
matters. She was a friendly, self-sufficient, kindly woman of
Irish stock, vigorous for her fifty-four years. Once knowing her,
one was struck by her persevering, energetic temperament that
obviously needed some kind of outlet. After her husband died in
1946, and there were no children, she adopted (not legally) and
made a home for several orphaned youths in their teens who
worked near her house in a Los Angeles suburb. She explained
why: "Happiness is Heaven; I'm happy in trying to do for others."

"My earliest memory was the day they put my dad in his
grave," she recounted. "Mother used to tell me I tried to jump

* Constructed from a series of personal interviews totaling approximately eighteen hours.

in after him. I can still see that today." She was only two years old then, an only child. Three years later her mother remarried. Louise never liked her stepfather. "He drank," she said, "and I can't tolerate that in anybody. One day I had to go to the store to see that my stepfather, who was drunk, came home. I was so humiliated. . . . It was not a happy life, there was always tension in the household. One day my stepfather tried to kill my mother, or said he was going to, but I took the axe away from him."

During those years Louise lived on a farm in central California, but when she started to school, she went to town to stay with an aunt. This aunt was a Baptist, while Louise was born a Catholic. The aunt made her attend the local Baptist church. By the age of nine Louise had already decided that she did not like churches. Moreover, she felt that this aunt was "uppity," insisting on choosing Louise's playmates. "Well, I sneaked around the corner and played with the 'alley-rats,'" Louise disclosed. "A little colored girl was one of my best friends. I felt no race hatred. I don't know why some consider themselves better." When she was fourteen, her stepfather died. She quit school, got a job, and from that time on worked as a clerk, waitress, and cook.

An overview of her case shows that several events had sharp and almost traumatic impacts upon the personality of the child, Louise. First, there was her father's death with the customary ritual and undertaker's paraphernalia. Afterwards her family life was unhappy and she was glad to get away from it. She rebelled against the last person, her aunt, who tried to constrain her to a proper, middle-class pattern of behavior. During the years following, while working at different jobs, she read widely, and her choice was "everything along the line of religious, metaphysical, and economic thinking—no novels. . . . Books about serious things. . . . I've seen so many ragged people and cripples; I wanted to help them." Her religious interests were universal: "I attended any church. No, the Roman Catholic ritual doesn't appeal to me. And some of the Catholics are so narrow, I can't take that. . . . The only religion I have is the Golden Rule. My friends used to laugh when I told them that."

At twenty-eight she married a man of like mind and for twenty years enjoyed a happy marriage, ended by his accidental death, a great shock to her. "If it hadn't been for my metaphysical understanding, I don't know what I'd have done."

During the depression Louise and her husband had been destitute—without a job, barely able to pay rent, and often not knowing where the next meal was coming from. They had recuperated financially, however, by the time they heard of Mankind United, that crucial day coming in 1939. They read the textbook and immediately entered the movement. "I must have had thoughts of Mankind United in mind, because as soon as it came along, I knew that this is what we had been looking for. Maybe these thoughts came from another life. When I was a youngster, I felt I had seen things before—in another existence —I don't know why or how."

Because of her dedicated labors on behalf of the cult, she soon became a subofficial in a southern California bureau. Regular weekly meetings were held in her house with between twenty-five and twenty-seven people attending. "We felt we had a mission to bring a new day. It was really inspirational. No, nobody ever questioned the story of the Sponsors. We were so thrilled that we walked on air all the time. We were just waiting for the time when we could have the 30-day Program."

Her primary interest being the economics rather than the

religion of the cult, she lost much of her enthusiasm when the transition was made to Christ's Church. However, Louise and her husband, while not entering as full-time Student Ministers, devoted their Sundays to working on a project. She rebelled against the attempts to control the thoughts of the Student Ministers. "It seemed that after the Church was formed, things changed—'You do what I say, or else'—No one has the right to tell me that." Before long they withdrew from Christ's Church of the Golden Rule. Notwithstanding, even after leaving the cult Louise said, "I still believe in the ideals and principles of Mankind United. I always will. I probably would be in there now if it hadn't been for that broken promise in recording the deed to our house. It's too bad there aren't better leaders."

Notes

CHAPTER I

Of Myth, Miracles, and Utopia

1. *Mankind United, A Challenge to "Mad Ambition" and "The Money Changers" Accompanied by an Invitation to the World's "Sane" Men and Women.* (Published by The International Registration Bureau, Pacific Coast Division of North America, originally copyrighted in 1934. Fifth edition copyrighted in 1938), p. 25.
2. *Ibid.*, p. 4.
3. *Ibid.*, p. 5.
4. *Ibid.,.* p. 21.
5. *Ibid.*, p. 26.
6. *Ibid.*, p. 53-54.
7. *Ibid.*, p. 26.
8. *Would You Be Informed?* (Mankind United pamphlet, October 22, 1941), p. 11.
9. Jack B. Tenney Committee—Assembly Fact-Finding Committee on Un-American Activities in California. Testimony of December 1, 1941.
10. *In the Matter of Christ's Church of the Golden Rule, Inc., Bankrupt. Reporter's Transcript of Proceedings of June 21, 1946.* In Bankruptcy, No. 44,128-WM. Before Hon. Benno M. Brink, Referee in Bankruptcy, in the District Court of the United States for the Southern District of California, Central Division, p. 115.
11. *Department "A" Bulletin* (Mankind United Publication, July 4, 1944).
12. *Christ's Church, Bankrupt, Transcript* (June 21, 1946), pp. 116 ff.
13. *Tenney Committee Report,* pp. 1377 ff.
14. *Los Angeles Examiner* (April 8, 1943), Sec. II, p. 1.
15. *Which Do You Want? The Rule of Gold or the Golden Rule?* (Mankind United Publication, February, 1941).
16. *Los Angeles Daily News* (March 25, 1944), p. 2.
17. *Los Angeles Herald Express* (March 25, 1944), p. 5.
18. *Los Angeles Daily News* (March 25, 1944), p. 2.
19. *Los Angeles Herald Express* (December 4, 1941), p. 2.
20. *Order to Show Cause.* In the Matter of Christ's Church of the Golden Rule, No. 44,128-WM in Bankruptcy. In the District Court of the United States, Southern District of California, Central Division (July 16, 1946), p. 5.
21. *Tenney Committee Report,* pp. 1409 ff.
22. *Mankind United,* p. 204.
23. *Ibid.,* pp. 204-205.
24. *From "The Speaker" in Behalf of The International Institute of Universal Research and Administration To All Registrants who have retained their love for, and faith in, the Christly vision eluci-*

dated in the textbook, "Mankind United." (December 21, 1951), pp. 20-21.

25. *Mankind United*, p. 88.
26. *Order to Show Cause*. In the Matter of Christ's Church, Bankrupt (July 16, 1946), p. 4.
27. *Mankind United*, p. 37.
28. *Ibid.*, p. 17.
29. *Ibid.*, pp. 9-10.
30. *Ibid.*, p. 105.
31. *Ibid.*, pp. 104-106.
32. *Ibid.*, pp. 107-108.
33. Notes on Mankind United "International 4-4-8-3-4 Club" Meeting (1938).
34. Notes on Mankind United Section Meeting (May 19, 1942).
35. *Tenney Committee Report*, p. 1457.
36. Notes on Mankind United Section Meeting (May 19, 1942).
37. *Would You Be Informed?* (Mankind United Pamphlet, October 22, 1941).
38. *Mankind United*, p. 59.
39. *Ibid.*, pp. 223-225, and *passim*.
40. *Ibid.*, p. 122.
41. *Ibid.*, p. 123.
42. *Ibid.*, pp. 44-48.
43. *Ibid.*, p. 219.
44. *Ibid.*, p. 239.
45. *Weekly Message* (April 8, 1944), p. 3.

CHAPTER II

The Pacific Coast Division of the International Registration Bureau of Mankind United

1. *Mankind United*, p. 267.
2. *Ibid.*
3. Personal interview.

4. "Can Mr. Bell Ring Up His Pixies?" *The American Weekly* (June 4, 1944), p. 17.
5. *A Proclamation for All Registrants* (May, 1939), p. 2.
6. *Tenney Committee Report* (March 20, 1944), pp. 125 ff.
7. *Order to Show Cause*, Christ's Church, Bankrupt (July 16, 1946), p. 25.
8. *Christ's Church, Bankrupt, Transcript* (January 24, 1947).
9. Personal interview.
10. Personal interview.
11. Personal interview (September 9, 1954).
12. *Instructions to all Bureau Managers* (n.d.).
13. *Los Angeles Examiner* (March 24, 1944), Sec. II, p. 1.
14. *Word to Incoming Chairmen* (Mankind United Publication, n.d.), p. 1.
15. *Los Angeles Herald Express* (March 20, 1944), p. 6.
16. *Tenney Committee Report* (May 22, 1942), p. 3191.
17. *Christ's Church, Bankrupt, Transcript* (January 24, 1947), Mr. Bell testifying.
18. *Los Angeles Examiner* (December 19, 1942), p. 3.
19. *Los Angeles Examiner* (March 20, 1944), p. 1.
20. *Christ's Church, Bankrupt, Transcript* (August 8, 1946), Judge Benno M. Brink speaking, p. 21.

CHAPTER III

Christ's Church of the Golden Rule

1. Miscellaneous excerpts from the cult literature of early 1944.

2. *Department "A" Telegram* (Mankind United Publication, June 5, 1943), p. 4.

3. *Instructions #1 for those going on projects* (Mankind United Publication, December 25, 1943), p. 1.

4. *Los Angeles Examiner* (March 20, 1944), p. 1.

5. *Los Angeles Herald Express* (March 25, 1944), p. 5.

6. *Department "A" Bulletin* (July 4, 1944), pp. 11-12.

7. The principal source of this list is the *Auditors' Report* for Christ's Church, Bankrupt (Arthur Young & Company, Los Angeles, California, June 28, 1946).

8. *Christ's Church, Bankrupt, Transcript* (August 8, 1946), pp. 28-29.

9. *Ibid.*, (June 14, 1946), p. 21.

10. *Ibid.*, (June 14, 1946), p. 22.

11. Personal interview.

12. *Christ's Church, Bankrupt, Transcript* (June 21, 1946), pp. 26-27.

13. A total of 819 members and ex-members actually filed claims against the bankrupt estate of Christ's Church of the Golden Rule. However, a small number who became Student Ministers failed to file claims, hence the estimate of 850.

14. Information obtained by examining claims filed against the bankrupt estate of Christ's Church.

15. *Weekly Message* (October 26, 1946), p. 3.

16. *Los Angeles Examiner* (March 20, 1944), p. 3.

17. *Instructions #1 for those going on projects* (December 25, 1943), p. 3.

18. *Weekly Message* (June 23, 1945), p. 2.

19. *Christ's Church, Bankrupt, Transcript* (June 18, 1946), p. 87.

20. *Ibid.*, (June 18, 1946), p. 75.

21. Personal interview.

22. *Christ's Church, Bankrupt, Transcript* (March 14, 1946), p. 70.

23. *Ibid.*

24. *From "The Speaker" in Behalf of The International Institute of Universal Research and Administration To All Registrants who have retained their love for, and faith in, the Christly vision elucidated in the textbook, "Mankind United."* (December 21, 1951), p. 4.

25. *Ibid.*, p. 10.

26. *Ibid.*, pp. 7-8.

27. *Ibid.*, p. 6.

28. *Ibid.*, pp. 6-7

29. *Ibid.*, p. 10.

30. *Ibid.*, p. 21.

31. *Ibid.*, p. 14.

32. *Ibid.*, p. 17.

CHAPTER IV

"The Voice of the Right Idea"

1. *Christ's Church, Bankrupt, Transcript* (June 12, 1946), p. 40.

2. Many cultists personally have aired these sentiments to the author.

3. Personal interview with the author (April 26, 1947).

4. *Department "A" Bulletin* (July 4, 1944), p. 9.

5. *Tenney Committee Report* (March 22, 1944).

6. Personal interview (April 26, 1947).

7. *Ibid.*

8. *Department "A" Bulletin* (July 4, 1944), p. 9.
9. State Hearing (Attorney General's office, May 11, 1945).
10. *Department "A" Bulletin* (July 4, 1944), p. 9.
11. *Ibid.*, p. 5.
12. *Ibid.*, p. 10.
13. *Ibid.*, p. 8.
14. *Ibid.*, p. 5.
15. *Christ's Church, Bankrupt, Transcript* (June 21, 1946), p. 115.
16. *Department "A" Bulletin* (July 4, 1944), p. 10.
17. *Ibid.*, p. 5.
18. *Ibid.*, p. 6.
19. *Tenney Committee Report* (December 2, 1941), pp. 1497 ff.
20. *Order to Show Cause*, Christ's Church, Bankrupt (July 16, 1946), p. 6.
21. *Tenney Committee Report* (December 1, 1941), pp. 1374 ff.
22. *Ibid.*, pp. 1409 ff.
23. *Ibid.*, pp. 1456 ff.
24. Personal interview with a former member who had attended the cult meeting.
25. *Speaker's Remarks Made at County Supervisors' Conference* (January 18, 1943), p. 5.
26. Quotations from the author's personal interviews with various former members.
27. Personal interview (April 26, 1947).
28. State Hearing (Attorney General's office, May 11, 1945).
29. *From "The Speaker" in Behalf of The International Institute of Universal Research and Administration To All Registrants who have retained their love for, and faith in, the Christly vision elucidated in the textbook, "Mankind United."* (December 21, 1951), p. 22.
30. *Ibid.*, p. 23.

CHAPTER V

Uniter of Mankind

1. Carey McWilliams, *Southern California Country* (New York, 1946), p. 370.
2. *Mankind United*, p. 310.
3. *We Are Not Cattle!* (Mankind United Publication, May, 1941).
4. *The Time is Short* (Anonymous, published by the International Registration Bureau of Mankind United, 1937), p. 74.
5. *Weekly Message* (March 17, 1945), p. 3.
6. *Ibid.*, p. 3.
7. *Mankind United*, p. 236.
8. *Ibid.*, p. 187.
9. Personal interview.
10. *Ibid.*
11. *Ibid.*
12. *Ibid.*
13. *Ibid.*
14. *Ibid.*
15. *Ibid.*
16. Notes on Mankind United Section Meeting (August 17, 1942).
17. Data obtained from personal interviews and Christ's Church Application-for-Membership forms.
18. Personal interview.
19. *Ibid.*
20. *The Old Order Passeth* (Mankind United Publication, 1939).
21. *Speaker's Remarks* (Mankind United Publication, October 25, 1942), p. 12.
22. *Merriam-Webster's Collegiate Dictionary.*
23. Notes on Mankind United Section Meeting (June 2, 1942).
24. *Ibid.* (April 18, 1942).
25. *Ibid.* (February 28, 1942).
26. Student Minister digest, "What is Man?" (n.d.).

27. Personal interview.
28. *Ibid.*
29. *Ibid.*
30. *Which Are You Choosing?* (Mankind United Publication, n.d.), p. 1.
31. *Thinking Humanity* (Mankind United Publication, n.d.), p. 1.
32. In numerous personal interviews.
33. Personal interview.
34. *Ibid.*
35. *Notes to Captains* (Mankind United Publication, 1939).

36. *Instructions to Captains and Lieutenants of the "Ray-of-Light" Bureau* (Mankind United Publication, March, 1940), p. 1.
37. *Weekly Message* (October 5, 1946), p. 3.
38. Personal interview.
39. *Ibid.*
40. *Ibid.*
41. *Ibid.*
42. Sample opinions cited at random from personal interviews.

Index

Abundance, Law of, 126
Adam dream of materiality, 122, 130
Adjustment, Law of, 126
Anglo-Israelites, 97
Anomie, 134, 149-150
Anti-capitalism, 111
Appeals of the cult, ix, x, 105-107
Aquarian Age, 98
Armageddon, 15, 130, 150
Astrology: ascending planes in, 124
Atlantis, 1, 125
Atom bombs, 72, 130
Attorney General of California, 66, 136
Auras, 124

Bankruptcy proceedings: as a legal battle, 66-68; destructive impact, 70-71; effect on cult prophet, 94; as source of information, 136, 139
Battle Hymn of Mankind United, 37
Bell, Arthur L.: as a Vigilante, 6; early accounts of, 6, 84; prophetic call, 7, 82-83; powers of translevitation, 10-11; at early meetings, 29; technique of cult leadership, 38-39, 91-92; as Church Trustee, 49, 54, 64; as Senior Elder, 70; as "The Speaker," 70-75 *passim*; prophetic message, 72, 92; concerning rebirth, 75; exodus from cult scene, 75; personal sacrifices, 77; prophetic role, 78; official titles and aliases, 79; as Christian Scientist, 80, 81; early life, 80; education, 80-81; business interests, 82; marriages, 82, 83; and news reporters, 87; personal description, 87-88, 91; and night clubs, 88-89; manner of living, 89-90; as a speaker, 90-92; cultic reaction to, 92, 149; style of writing,

92-93; attitude toward theology, 93; during bankruptcy trial, 94; farewell message, 94-95; as a metaphysician, 120; and ex-members, 131. *See also* Division Superintendent
Bellamy, Edward: *Looking Backward*, 27, 81; *Equality*, 27, 81; rumors of, 110
Biblical prophecy, 128
Black magic, 124, 127
Bryan, William Jennings, 145
Bureau Managers, 30, 38
Bureaus: early form of, 30; in Los Angeles, 31; "Ruth-Ann," 31-32; spread of, 31; alongside church projects, 55-56; "Ray of Light," 129

California Legislative Fact-finding Committee on Un-American Activities, 9, 11, 41, 49, 83-84, 86
California scene, 81-82
Captains, 30-31
Case studies: use of, 133
Cause and Effect, Law of, 126
Chiropractors, 101
Christian Science, 80, 81, 98, 120
Christ's Church of the Golden Rule: incorporation of, 44-45; and Mankind United, 45; early financial drive, 46-47; Articles of Incorporation, 47-48; as Universal Service Corporation, 47; By-Laws of, 53; Canon Laws of, 70; Ecclesiastical Society of, 70; metaphysics, 121, 128; and world crisis, 130
Church projects: assignments to, 38, 57; establishing of, 49, 53; conditions on, 57-58, 59-60, 65, 109; secrecy on, 57; camaraderie on,

137; subsequent reaction to, 145, 148
Matter, 120
Members. *See Cult individual*
Meniketti, Orlando: testimony of, 83-84
Mentalphysics, 97, 124
Messianic Age, 129
Metaphysics: the message of, 120-128 *passim;* defined, 120-122; and Universal Law, 122; place of error, 123; theory of vibrations, 123-124; appeal of, 127-128
Millennium, 46, 55, 128-129
Money-changers: outrage at, 106
Motivations: levels of, 133-134

New Age, 128, 129
New Race groups, 96, 98
New Thought, 97, 120
Nordskott, Mrs. Adelaide P., 75

Oahspe Bible, 97
Orthodox churches: reaction to, 36, 111, 112
Orthodoxy: attitude toward, 115, 144-145

Proclamation for All Registrants, 36
Progress, Law of, 130
Project Managers: examples of, 63, 65; importance of, 65; cultist's reaction to, 149
Properties: description of, 49-53 *passim;* Southern California, 50-51; Northern California, 52-53; Oregon, 53
Prophecy, 129
Psychological mechanisms, 133
Pyramidology, ix, 97

Quotas, 38

Registrant, 31
Reincarnation: idea of, 124-125
Relations with the outer world, 56-57, 65-71 *passim*
Religion of the Stars, 98

Religious Preludes, 111-117 *passim*
Research materials: sources of, 136-137
Rosicrucians, 97

Schism in cult ranks, 64-65
Secrecy toward outsiders, 140
Sedition trial: of Mankind United leaders, 43-44
Sermon on the Mount, 126
Sin, 122
Spiritualism, 97
Sponsors: origin of, 2; anonymity of, 3; executive board of, 3; cult program of, 5; relaying system of, 7; renounce the planet Earth, 72; proof of, 78; appointment of Bell by, 81; call to arms, 104; cultist's reaction to, 148
Statistical Project 11-A: function of, 53, 60
Student Ministers: early drive for, 47, 54-55; placement of, 53; number of, 56; financial contributions of, 56; relations with the outer world, 56-57, 107; as crusaders, 57-58; camaraderie of, 57, 59-60; recompense received, 59; dissenters among, 66; appeal of metaphysics, 121, 127-128; loyal remnant of, 131. *See also Cult individual*

Technocrats, 97
Ten Commandments, 126
Textbook. *See Mankind United*
Theosophy, 97, 120
"30-day Program": nature of, 5, 22; and Hidden Rulers, 21-22; release of, 21, 71; audience for, 22; Election Supervisors for, 22, 40; to stop war, 42; as millennium, 129
Townsend Plan, 97
Translevitation: explanation of, 10-11, 124; to other planets, 74; powers of cult leader, 86-87

Unity, 97, 120
Universal Laws: concept of, 122,
129; and health, 125; list of, 126;
appeal of, 128
Universal Service Corporation: establishment of, 5, 21, 36, 71, 119;
monument to, 12; as the "City of
Brotherhood," 20, 132; described,
20-27 *passim;* and 30-day Program, 21; sense of mission, 21;
benefits of, 23-24; executive board
of, 23; utopian life in, 24-26;
limited-use money, 25; and world-
wide militia, 26-27; education in,
26; international auxiliary language, 26; and Edward Bellamy,
27; and Golden Rule, 27; as
Christ's Church of the Golden
Rule, 46, 55; other-planetary pattern of, 73, 74, 76; news reports
about, 98
Utopia. *See* Universal Service Corporation

Vegetarianism, 124
Verstehen, 134
Vibrations: theory of, 74, 123-124,
125
Views and Variations, 117-120 *pas-
sim*

War: cultic view of, 35, 36
Weber, Max, 133
World-Savers, 103-111 *passim*
World War II: cultic interpretation
of, 19, 39; effect on meetings, 40

Yoga, 97